From Silence to Secrecy

A Memoir

MARTHA E. LEIKER

iUniverse, Inc.
Bloomington

From Silence to Secrecy
A Memoir

iUniverse books may be ordered through booksellers or by contacting:

iUniverse
1663 Liberty Drive
Bloomington, IN 47403
www.iuniverse.com
1-800-Authors (1-800-288-4677)

ISBN: 978-1-45027-748-8 (pbk)
ISBN: 978-1-45027-749-5 (cloth)
ISBN: 978-1-45027-750-1 (ebk)

Library of Congress Control Number: 2010918104

Printed in the United States of America

iUniverse rev. date: 12/3/2010

Disclaimer

All statements of fact, opinion, or analysis expressed are those of the author and do not reflect the official positions or views of the CIA or any other United States government agency. Nothing in the contents should be construed as asserting or implying United States government authentication of information or agency endorsement of the author's views. This material has been reviewed by the CIA to prevent the disclosure of classified information.

I have not embellished nor created facts to enhance the stories, but based this book on facts as I remembered them. I attempted for the reader's benefit to write in an interesting and informative manner. A brief historical summary of some countries or states in which I have resided are included.

Acknowledgments

In loving memory of my parents,
my twin sister Mary,
Sig. Jr., and Linus.

Dad   Mom

Mary Sig. Jr. Linus (Josh)

Contents

Preface

My life has been like that of a chameleon—changing from one lifestyle to another. As a young girl, I dreamed about working in Africa with the African people. To accomplish this goal, I entered a convent to become a missionary sister, but life's challenges changed my direction, and years later, I found myself working for the Central Intelligence Agency (CIA). I have spoken about the various phases of my life to many people and was always told to write a book.

Writing this book brought back many memories from my childhood on a Kansas farm, to Pennsylvania, where I trained as a nun, followed by work for the CIA in Virginia and in Africa. My legacy to the reader is to show that a young girl with a dream can accomplish much, even though my dream took a twist and changed radically.

For the last ten years, writing this book has been an ongoing process. While attending many of the National Active and Retired Federal Employees Association (NARFE) chapter meetings during the past years, I have given presentations on my life. I will explain more about this organization later. Now others have the opportunity to share in my life experiences.

Introduction

My story begins on a Kansas farm in the 1940s when my twin sister Mary and I were born. It was during this time that World War II pulled us out of the Great Depression. Farm life was difficult. My parents worked from dawn until dusk to ensure their family of six children was taken care of as well as times would allow.

In the late 1950s, the family moved to Colorado Springs, where my sisters and I finished high school. The nuns who had taught me in grade school and high school had a lasting effect on me, displayed by their dedication and devotion. I looked up to those sisters and admired them but didn't want to join their order. Sometimes I thought they were too strict, but they were the voice of authority. The seed that was planted in my soul in childhood to become a nun remained with me for many years. I believed God was calling me to work with his people in Africa. Why Africa?

Whenever I had to write a term paper or essay, the subject was always Africa. I loved researching that continent, which pulled me like a magnet, and couldn't satisfy the desire to work with its people. The people and their lifestyles were so totally new to me, and I wanted to find out for myself. There was no question in my mind that the religious life was my vehicle to attain my goal. At the time, it seemed that the only way to reach my destination to serve in Africa was to join a religious order, so I researched many orders and found one that sent their sisters only to Africa. I knew that if I joined this particular order, I would be destined to go to Africa and nowhere else.

A French Cardinal, the founder of this order, had convents throughout Europe and some convents in the United States, so I figured there were some Americans in the order. My quest for adventure required boarding a train to Pennsylvania to begin training for religious life. After eight years, the order assigned my first mission in Africa. Zambia was my first assignment, and I spent eight years working there with the people. After a short stay in Frascati, Italy, I returned to the States and left the order.

My path then led to the Central Intelligence Agency (CIA) to begin work at their headquarters in Virginia. I completed a year of training, and I was sent again to work in Africa. All of this transpired because I had gone down to one of the government buildings in Denver to get an application to work for the government. I picked up the application, and as I walked out of the building, I noticed a poster on the bulletin board with Uncle Sam in his tri-colored hat pointing his finger at me. The caption read, "I NEED YOU." In smaller letters, it stated the CIA was looking for people to work in Africa. The word "Africa" stood out. I knew immediately I was going back to Africa. After all this time, I wasn't sure what the CIA was because, when I was in Africa as a nun, I was twenty-six, and I didn't keep up with American news. As things worked out, I spent another six years in Africa as a government worker.

During the last remaining years before retirement, I worked at the HQS building in Virginia.

My home is now in Denver, Colorado, where I am serving as a regional vice president for the National Active and Retired Federal Employees Association (NARFE), which protects the rights and benefits of the federal worker, retiree, and survivor annuitant. It's the only organization formed to accomplish this goal. There are nationwide chapters including the District of Columbia, Panama, the Philippines, the Virgin Islands, and Puerto Rico. NARFE membership totals 309,000.

The region I cover comprises Arizona, Colorado, New Mexico, Utah, and Wyoming, with seventeen thousand members. Traveling to these states is a must in order to attend executive board meetings and district training meetings as well as state conventions. As regional vice president, I conduct a regional conference in one of the five states. The conference is an opportunity to learn the latest information concerning congressional actions that affect the organization and presents opportunities for leadership training.

My daily life is taken up with answering phone calls and e-mails and generally acting as a liaison between the eighty-six chapters, five federations, and our national headquarters. This necessitates travel to Alexandria, Virginia, to attend national executive board meetings.

Through the years, I came up through the ranks in a Denver chapter from chapter treasurer to chapter president and on to federation president, and for the past two years, I have served as regional vice president.

In August 2010 I was a candidate for the national vice president's position. I did not win the election but ran a close race. I have met many wonderful, dedicated people who inspired and encouraged me to share my life in writing.

Because my life has been so different from others and because I have faced many challenges through the years, especially in Africa, I decided to put it all down on paper and share it with others.

My roots stem from the Leikers in the United States, who are all descendants of the German-Russian settlers from the Volga Region in Russia, who settled in Ellis County in Kansas. Our Germanic background may explain the reason we are strong survivors, as evidenced in my changing life.

My grandfather was nine years old when he and his brothers traveled from Germany to the United States. His brothers settled in Munjor, Kansas, while Grandpa settled in Victoria, where he raised horses. Ahead of the times, he played the stock market and became one of the wealthiest people in Ellis County.

The German spelling for our name is Leicker, but the Russian spelling is Leiker, which remains today. German was the language spoken at my paternal grandparents' home, so communication with my grandparents was limited for us children.

My grandmother always made us feel welcome and, in her kindly way, spoke to us even though we couldn't understand her. Grandpa, a tall man, watched us but didn't say much and rarely smiled.

Mom, an attractive woman, was five foot four. She was also of German descent. She had light brown hair and a smile in her hazel eyes, and she was a friendly person. She made everyone feel welcome and loved. She didn't know anyone she couldn't befriend. Her eyes lit up when her children walked into the room. Dad, a quiet man, was six foot two. He always had a cigarette in his mouth and did not show emotion outwardly.

My three older brothers were Sig "Siggie" Jr., Leroy "Buster," and Linus "Linny." When Mary and I were born, Siggie was ten years older than us. Leroy was eight years older and Linus was seven years older than we were. When they were joined by us, they learned some new duties by taking care of us, but they weren't always happy about it.

Martha and Mary

Our younger sister, Armina "Minny," who was my mother's namesake, followed eighteen months later. Dad and my three brothers worked on the six hundred and forty acre Palmer Farm, our home that our Grandpa had purchased.

True to our German heritage, my family survived the rigors of farm living, getting up early to feed the cows, horses, and other farm animals, surviving the dust storms, the drought, and the hardships of daily life. In Hays proper, we survived a flood, even though we lost everything. My life depicted my strong German heritage when I left the family at an early age and went through disciplined training, which eventually led to life in Africa, serving the people amid a challenging environment. When a life change came my way again, the inner fortitude to follow another way of life helped me to once again begin a new life in Africa, working for the government under very different circumstances.

Mary and Martha

Martha, Mary, Mom, and Minny

Lee, Mary, Martha, and Linus

Chapter 1

KANSAS, 1940

Black and blue at birth, my twin sister was immediately baptized as Mary. Mom and Dad named us after the two sisters in the Bible, Mary and Martha. It was during harsh times, in Hays, Kansas, on January 10, 1940, at eleven-thirty in the morning that I came into the world, with my twin sister following ten minutes later. Family and friends were all smiles as they received the two cigars my Dad handed out instead of the usual one.

Life on the farm was demanding and called for many sacrifices. It took a lot of work to keep it going and to keep the farm animals fed and watered.

LIFE ON THE FARM

The sun hadn't come up yet, but Dad and my brothers headed out to the barn, which smelled of straw and cow manure. They sat on small stools next to the cows and drew out the milk into buckets held between their legs. The cows' tails swished away the flies, sometimes hitting them in the face.

"Siggie, look," Buster would say. Squirt, squirt. "Linny, you're next." Squirt, squirt.

Buster, the culprit, got his share next.

When the milking was finished and the cows were let out to pasture, Dad and the boys returned to the house carrying the buckets of milk. Mom separated the cream from the milk. Her butter from the cream found its way onto many sandwiches or onto her delicious baked bread. She prepared a hearty breakfast consisting of fried eggs, bacon or ham from our pigs that had been slaughtered, freshly baked bread, and strong black coffee. When Dad and the boys left to do daily chores, she made substantial sandwiches of baked ham or roast beef on a bed of lettuce leaves topped with large tomato slices. Her garden was a sea of fresh tomatoes, peppers, cucumbers, potatoes, and whatever seeds she could get to grow. Her green thumb proved productive because whatever she planted always came up. She canned fruits and vegetables and pickled cucumbers, so the pantry was never empty.

In the early mornings, Mom would rouse us girls, at ages four and five, from sleep and say, "C'mon, girls, it's time to do the chores. Let's go."

Dressed in our homemade dresses, we weren't always that willing to go, but we had no choice, so with our buckets of feed, we threw seed to the hungry chickens, geese, turkeys, and guinea fowl.

"Mary, throw your seed over here to these chickens. Martha, go over to the other side and get those chickens. Minny, watch out for the geese."

The geese on the other side came running with their long necks bobbing up and down, threatening us to come nearer.

Mom said, "Look, how they come for the food."

The wild turkeys also sauntered over for food. When we finished with the chickens, we lugged buckets of food over to the pig pen.

"Come on, let's go to the pigs. They're waiting for us because they're hungry too," I said.

As we neared their pen, they ran to us, snorting and squealing, to chomp on the corn husks and leftovers we put in their feed trough. The three of us, in our pig tails, laughed and watched them wallow in the mud.

"Mary, look at the pigs," Minny said.

"I see them. They're so dirty and funny."

About every other day Mom baked fresh bread, so the aroma of freshly baked bread tipped the nose of all in the house. The cinnamon rolls she made were a daily delight for the family. She loved to cook, so we ate delicious healthy meals consisting of meat, potatoes, and vegetables. From her garden, we enjoyed fresh tomatoes, carrots, lima beans, peas, lettuce, string beans, and potatoes.

Dad and the boys headed out into the fields to repair fences, complete daily tasks in the field, or repair the combines or other farm equipment. After a long day's work when Dad and the boys returned to the house, Mom sauntered over to the counter where they had put their lunch boxes, opened the empty black lunch boxes, and commented, breaking into a smile, beaming from ear to ear, "I see you cleaned out your boxes. You must have been hungry."

Gratitude was not mentioned but understood.

"We sure were," Leroy said.

Siggie, at age fifteen, babysat us a lot when Mom and Dad had to go into town for supplies or to visit friends. My other two brothers helped but usually found something else to do. Siggie, gentle and easy-going, made it easy for us to do what he told us.

"Girls, what do you want to do?" he asked.

"We'll play with our dolls." His face broke into a smile, and he was glad that we contented ourselves with our dolls. His kind manner instilled trust as he kept an eye on us. Buster and Linny took turns putting us girls in a cardboard box and dragging us around the yard.

Minny decided to take her little doll to the outhouse with her and sat her on the second hole. The doll slipped and fell into the hole. Minny came out crying that her doll had fallen in. She pleaded with the boys to get it for her and couldn't understand why they wouldn't go in and get her doll. She cried a lot about losing her doll.

Daily life took its toll. Weather dictated crop survival. The hot, dry summers challenged Dad and my brothers when they were riding on the combines harvesting the wheat. Sweat glands worked overtime forcing droplets to roll off their faces. There were no air-conditioned cabs on the combines in those times, so thick dust penetrated their clothing as evidenced by the dark water on laundry days.

Around the house, Mom used an old wringer washing machine and enlisted our help to hang the clothes on the outside clothesline that Dad had installed.

She said, "Mary and Martha, help me carry the basket of clothes to the line. Minny, hand me the clothes pins."

Minny held the bag of clothes pins, took one out, and handed it to Mom. Mom pinned the wet clothes on the line. The hot dry wind pushed them back and forth, making them sway in the fresh air and sunshine that permeated them with the "outdoors" scent. Sometimes Mom got us mixed up and called us by the wrong names, but she made sure we did our share of the work.

The evening stillness overshadowed the land when the huge, orange sun ball veiled the peacefulness of the land as it dipped into the shadows and the animals settled in for the night.

The boys helped Dad most of the time when they weren't in school, and we girls helped Mom in the kitchen or cleaned the house. We took turns doing the dishes, but it was a fight sometimes. One of us always felt it was the other's turn to do the dishes.

"Minny, it's your turn for the dishes," I said.

"No, it isn't. I did them last night." One of us ended up doing the dishes whether we liked it or not.

Dad and the neighbor alternated taking the boys and the neighbor kids to school. Dad had to keep a stern hand on the boys because they weren't always so helpful but got into trouble riding the pigs or riding the calves.

"Let's go find a calf to ride," Leroy said, and off they went. When Dad found out about their riding the calves, he spoke a few choice words that wouldn't let them forget about their escapade.

On another occasion the boys ran after the pigs, which snorted and grunted until they were exhausted and fell over. Dad wasn't too happy with the boys, and they got their share of punishment.

"Let's go to the creek for a swim," Linus said.

"Okay, let's go," Leroy replied.

"Maybe we should tell Mom we're going," Siggie said.

"C'mon, let's go," Linus answered. So off they went to the creek.

In the wintertime, the house was usually cold because there was no central heat. Heavy feather tick covers kept us warm during the cold nights. The boys carried in wood, so Mom put pieces of wood in the stove and let them burn to heat the house. The wood stove in the kitchen helped to keep that room warm, but the rest of the house was cold.

Whenever neighbors came over, we were all there to greet them.

"Dad, get your violin and play for us," Mom said.

It didn't take much for Dad to get out his violin, and his magic fingers danced on the violin strings. We sang the songs as best we could because they were usually in German. I think it was Dad who instilled the love of music in us. He not only played the violin but loved the organ and finally got one when we moved to Colorado Springs, which he played as much as time would allow when he returned home from work and on weekends. My oldest brother, Siggie, played in bands and orchestras and directed bands later in his life. Mary and I played the piano, and I took up bassoon and alto-saxophone later on. Minny also played the piano for a while. Mom played the piano a little and also played Dad's organ. She loved to sing along with us.

We didn't have much luxury on the farm, but we had a united family who worked together. We knew we had to help with the chores to get the work done. Fond memories of the farm remain with me today from life on the farm at age five.

Dad's parents lived in Walker, a town about sixteen miles down the road. We learned a few words in German but only a few. During our visits with them, Grandma, a small woman with a long black dress covering her slight body and big smile, said, "Girls, would you like some chocolates?"

"Yes, Grandma, we would," we answered, with big smiles on our small faces.

Often times Dad's brothers and sisters and their families, who were scattered in small towns around Walker, would all come together and reminisce about things they had done as children. Many faces broke into smiles, and laughter was heard through the house.

My maternal grandparents lived in a large, white house in Hays. Grandpa was a big, robust man. Grandma had her gray hair drawn into a bun on the back of her head. When they babysat us three girls, Grandma's high-pitched voice woke us up. She said, "Girls, it's time to get up. Your breakfast is ready." Her aging face broke into a smile when we came into the kitchen.

"Good morning, Grandma and Grandpa."

Grandma, in her long dress, which was topped with an apron, brought the eggs over to the table in the pan in which they were fried, the grease swirling around. "I hope you're hungry because you have to eat all these eggs," she said.

We sat down at the wooden table and looked at the breakfast with our eyes roving back and forth to each other because the egg yokes stared at us, daring us to eat them. Grandma didn't believe in turning eggs over when she fried them. To please Grandma, I closed my eyes and ate the watery eggs. Grandpa, a tall robust man, began eating with gusto. I guess he was hungry and was used to eggs staring at him. My eggs today are always turned over during frying.

To keep the farm productive and viable, Dad worked at the Walker Air Force Base as the post engineers' maintenance supervisor. Making ends meet necessitated his working two jobs, leaving precious little time to spend with the family.

Dad set up a small shop in the kitchen coop and made things out of wood. He didn't like farm work, so when he and Mom decided to move into town, Dad sold the farm, and preparations were made to move. Dad wanted to set up his own shop in town to work with wood.

Our Move to Hays, Kansas

In 1945, the family moved into Hays proper, where Dad set up his woodworking shop. He had limited education, but with his magic hands, he could make anything out of wood. Much of his work, such as chairs, tables, beds, vanities, and kitchen cabinets, found its way into surrounding houses. Churches also proved to be a resting place for his work in the pews he sawed, shaved, and sandpapered until they were perfect. Nothing went out of his shop until it passed his approval.

Minny, Dad, Mary, and Martha in front of Dad's shop

The house we moved into was not a completed house, but it had a roof on top of the basement. It was called a "basement house." The upstairs had not yet been built, so our daily living was spent in the basement, where we had three bedrooms, one bath, a living room, a dining room, a kitchen, and a storage room off the kitchen.

Martha, Mary, and Minny in front of basement house

For a period of eight years, we lived in this basement until 1953, when Dad made enough money to finish the house. Neighbors and relatives came from all over to help put up the frames and finish the work on the upstairs. During this time my oldest brother, Sig Jr., was away serving in the United States Navy. His wife, Lois, moved in with us to attend Fort Hays State College. She was a proficient musician and played the alto saxophone. At the time, I was taking lessons on the alto saxophone and bassoon and played in the grade school band and orchestra.

"Martha, let's play this piece together," Lois said.

"Okay, do you want me to play the bottom part or the top?"

"I'll play the melody, and you play the second part," she said.

She instilled some of her enthusiasm in me for these instruments by having us play duets together, which made me feel proud to play with a "musician." While I practiced, and I practiced a lot, I'm sure a lot of my wrong notes were hard on Mom's ears while she was cleaning or preparing a meal. At times I heard Mom call, "Martha, it's time to help make dinner. Come and help."

"Okay, I'll be right there." Often, I pretended not to hear because I was busy practicing.

After homework was done, Mary, Minny, and I often went outside to play baseball with a neighbor boy named Kenny. If he wasn't outside, one of us whistled until he came out of his home. The times he wanted to play, he would come over and whistle for us to come out. Our means of communication worked very well. We got our exercise and had fun at the same time.

To go to school, the three of us girls walked a few blocks to the grade school carrying our books. We didn't have school bags then, so we carried our books in our arms. After a few blocks, our arms ached. I was constantly changing the books from arm to arm because they got heavier and heavier. The three of us girls were always together, so we never walked home from school alone.

In the wintertime Dad warmed up the pickup and drove us to school at his usual twenty-five miles an hour.

"Dad, we have to be at school before a quarter of eight," I said.

"You'll get there; don't worry," he said. "Let's get in the truck." We climbed into the cab of the pickup. Sometimes we wondered if we would ever arrive at school on time. Dad was never in a hurry.

Mom and Dad thought music would be beneficial to us, so a decision was made to purchase a piano. The three of us began the painful task of learning to play those black and white keys. There weren't too many fights to take turns because practicing became old very quickly.

"Mary, go and practice the piano," Mom said.

"Do I have to?"

"Yes, you and Martha have a duet to play next week."

"Let Martha practice."

"No," I said. "It's your turn."

"Oh, all right."

After some painful time and acquired skill, Mary and I played duets in recitals. We were always together.

My Desire to Become a Nun

At times in grade school, I had broached the subject of becoming a nun to my parents and really thought I was ready to leave after the eighth grade. The subject was not new in the family because Mom had a sister who was a nun, and Dad had a brother who was a priest. Both seemed happy when I mentioned it to them.

"You're too young to know what you want to do. Wait until after high school, and if you still want to leave for the convent, we won't prevent you."

"All right."

I was disappointed because I felt I was ready, but I agreed to their plan. I always had a fascination with Africa and thought of it often and wondered how long it would be before I could actually attain my goal. My desire to work in Africa was my dream. Africa was a continent that held great appeal for me. Where did this crazy idea come from? I don't know, but Africa was a subject I loved to think about

The nuns who taught me probably inspired my desire to become a nun. I think God planted the seed to follow him to serve his people in Africa, but I had to wait a bit longer.

As we grew older, my sisters and I attended a small girls' high school under the supervision of the nuns. Every day we donned our long, black and white uniforms. We all looked alike. The only thing that differentiated us was size or hair color or hairstyle. I had been used to looking alike because of Mary, my twin. Mom had always dressed Mary and me alike since we were babies. It wasn't always easy to find clothes the same style and color, and that's where disagreements came into play. We always had to decide together if we wanted something, but sometimes it didn't always work out that way. Sometimes she gave in, and sometimes I did. At times, Mom decided the three of us girls should dress alike and told everyone we were triplets.

"Mary, let's wear the green dress to church."

"No, I like the blue one."

"The green one looks better."

"No, it doesn't."

Sometimes, Mom had to intervene and make the decision because neither of us would give in. Disagreements about clothes were the usual daily spat, but we got over them.

My brothers attended the military academy under the administration of the Jesuits and were active in sports, especially football. They would walk to the school a mile away, or Dad would give them a ride, or their friends came along and gave them a ride. Sitting on the bleachers with the hot sun bearing down on us, we watched the boys play football games. The family joined hundreds of other families in rooting for the home team

"C'mon, Linus, run that ball!" I yelled.

"Yeah, they're winning," Mary said. Those games gave us a chance to look the boys over. My brothers loved football and played well. We became big fans and didn't miss their games at the academy.

DRIVING LESSONS

When Mary and I turned fourteen and a half years old, we wanted to learn how to drive. We pleaded, "Dad, teach us how to drive. We need to know. All our friends are learning."

"All right, I'll take you both out in the pickup." He took us on country dirt roads to learn how to drive with the stick shift.

"Martha, you go first," Mary said. She wanted to watch so she would know what to do when it was her turn.

Dad explained, "You put your left foot on the clutch, move the stick shift into neutral, and then first. The right foot should be free to step on the brake. When you go a few feet, shift into second and then into third."

Well, it looked easier than it was. I put my left foot on the clutch, tried to shift into neutral and then to first, but the gearshift made some strange noise until I found the right place to change gears.

"Now, watch the road and stay on your side. You see the shoulder on the right, gauge the right side of the pickup by that line," Dad said.

I drove a short distance then had to give my place to Mary, so she could have her turn.

Figuring out how to use the clutch and the gearshift made learning easy because there were always two of us having a lesson at the same time. I watched her when she was driving, and she watched me when it was my turn. It was like having two lessons instead of one.

"What did that sign say on the road?" Dad asked.

"What sign?" Mary asked.

After reaching a certain degree of proficiency on dirt roads, we were upgraded to drive on the highway. On tarmac, the pickup glided across the road. Dad made sure we saw all the signs on the road and asked after we had passed any sign.

"What color was that sign?" he asked. He made us keenly aware of everything on both sides of the road

After a few weeks of lessons, Mary and I took the test and passed. We soon became proud owners of temporary licenses. We got to use Dad's pickup, but he was always with us.

As the years passed, my two oldest brothers attended Fort Hays College. Sig joined the Navy, and Linus later joined the Army. Leroy got married, finished college, and began teaching.

THE FLOOD

During my sophomore year in high school in 1955, the rains were heavy, forcing some creeks and rivers to overflow. On one peaceful night, we found ourselves caught in the middle of a flash flood. The raging water forcefully broke in the windows of our basement house. The basement was filling up with water.

In the frenzy of the moment Dad yelled, "Get the girls up and get them up on the roof!"

Fear took over. We ran up the stairs, opened the front door, and Dad lifted us up onto the roof. Mom moved around us as best she could on the sloping roof.

"Girls, are you okay?" Mom asked. She gave us some blankets that Dad had hurriedly handed to her.

"We're okay." We covered up with the blankets because the rain pelted us, leaving everything and everyone drenched. While sitting on the roof, we heard screaming, as people were caught in the current and carried down the street.

Dad saw what was happening, so he and Linus tied ropes around their waists with the other end tied to a tree, waded into the swift current, and caught people as they desperately tried to save themselves. The current was so swift it dragged them down the road. It was too swift to fight. Once Dad and Linus pulled the people out of the current to safer water, they, too, climbed up onto the sloping roof to join the rest of us.

"There's room over here."

There weren't too many blankets to go around, but the people were safe. It wasn't easy to sit on this sloped roof, but it was better than being in the cold water. Rain continued to fall throughout the night. The wet blankets became heavy and uncomfortable, so most of them were put aside. Somehow Dad had managed to get my cat out and give it to me, so I held her tightly to keep her dry, which distracted me from the cold and the rain.

At dawn, we could see water was everywhere. The house was flooded, and Dad's shop was flooded, sights we gazed upon in disbelief as we sat on the roof. Gas pumps from gas stations down the road had broken, and the smell of gas was in the water. By late morning, Dad helped us all down from the roof, and we girls were carried on the backs of Dad and Linus for a half block to where the water was much lower and we could walk in it. Six feet of water in the house ruined everything. Mud had demolished the beautiful, sometimes dreaded piano. Whatever we owned was not worth keeping because it smelled of mud. All the machinery in my dad's shop had been ruined. Dad, his eyes sad and disbelieving, stared at his beautiful works of art, which were covered with mud. The machines that made his work easier stood soaked in water. Mom, with tears rolling down her cheeks as she searched for photo albums, uttered a cry when she found them mud-soaked.

"Dad, look at all our photos. They're ruined."

"Well, we can't do anything about it now."

All her dishes were covered with mud. She and Dad looked at each other and understood what had to be done. She came over to us girls.

"You're going to stay with some friends on their farm while we try to clean up the place."

"Can't we help?" Mary pleaded. It was too much to comprehend at the time. Seeing this complete devastation of our things was more than any of us could bear.

"No, it will be easier if we know you are taken care of and out of this mud."

We wanted to stay and help, but they wouldn't hear of it. But before we could go to this farm, we had to get hepatitis and tetanus shots. On the friends' farm, we spent the next few days experiencing the effects of fever and the consequences of the shots—arms swollen from the needles.

Some aid companies were not efficient then as they are now, and very little help was offered to our family. Dad and Mom, along with relatives, did their best to clean up the house and Dad's shop. Many hours were spent scrubbing down walls, scrubbing floors, and cleaning out the cabinets. Dishes and clothes were washed.

After a few months, life as we knew it didn't work anymore, so Mom and Dad and Linus packed up the pickup and Leroy's car and made several trips to Colorado Springs with our meager belongings.

COLORADO SPRINGS, COLORADO, 1955

Colorado Springs, a town situated with a backdrop of the Rocky Mountains, seemed like paradise. Colorado stands out, even among other western states that appear large and boxy on the map. It lies at the approximate center of what was once called the Great American Desert—midway between Canada and Mexico and the Pacific and the Mississippi. It sits on the world's greatest deposits of oil shale, an expensive source of fuel and one the federal government tried for a time to develop.

Getting used to the altitude took about two weeks in our new house. All our belongings were put in place. Mom had a new kitchen, and we had new bedrooms. All of us slept a lot and took it easy until our bodies adjusted.

"Girls, are you okay. Do you feel tired or do you want to eat something?"

"I'm hungry," Minny replied.

We always seemed to be hungry or sleepy. Mom was always concerned about us. Dad found work, so he was gone during the day. The annual income rose to $4,707.

We found a high school and had to register for the fall semester. Mary and I were starting our junior year in high school, and Minny started her sophomore year. The high school was co-ed, so that was going to be a big change for us.

It was a new beginning for all of us. Dad drove us to St. Mary's Catholic High School, where Mary and I joined many other teenage boys and girls for our junior year. It was the policy of the school to separate twins, so for the first time, we did not have the same classroom or the same classes. It was a strange experience not to be together all the time. We met at lunchtime and after class.

"Mary, how did your class go?"

"Oh, it's interesting. We sure get a lot of homework to do. Did you get a lot?"

"Yeah, I got a lot to do for all the classes."

The black and white uniforms become an outdated memory, happily forgotten. Blouses and skirts became our dress code.

Whenever Mary and I wanted the car to drag the main street, we'd go to Minny, who usually got whatever she wanted from Dad.

"Minny, go ask Dad for the car keys."

"No, you ask him."

"You get what you want."

"All right, but I get to go with you."

Dad rarely refused Minny. I think it was because she was the baby in the family she usually got whatever she wanted. We soon learned she was the key to whatever we wanted to get, so we took advantage of the fact more than once.

Our first experience with the existence of pizza came during these first years in Colorado Springs. The famous Pizza Hut took our orders many times with our friends. Gasoline was thirty cents a gallon, so dragging the main streets was the highlight of our young lives. When we got the car, we met our friends at the local drive-in and ordered Cokes and burgers with those luscious french fries.

Martha driving with Mary and Minny in back

In order to make some spending money, Mary and I began work at Penrose Hospital cleaning off patients' trays and doing the dishes. With this money, we could pay for the gas we used in Dad's car. The last year of high school was ending, so another important decision had to be made.

"Mary, we have to get some prom dresses," I said.

We decided that we would not get the same dress, so Mom took us shopping.

"I'm going to take this one, so don't take the same one," she said.

"I looked at the dress she chose and found something in a different style and color.

"What do you think about this one?"

"That looks nice. Does it fit you?"

We both bought nice gowns and had dates for the prom. We double dated but didn't stay together once we arrived at the dance. I could tell Mary was enjoying herself because she smiled a lot and was out on the dance floor most of the time. I also enjoyed the dance and thought it was a great way to end our final year.

As graduation came near, I finalized my decision to change my life. Matthew 9:37 reads, "The harvest is plentiful, but the workers are few."

"Mom and Dad, remember when I told you I wanted to become a nun? At the time, you told me I had to wait until after high school. Well, I still want to leave, and now is the time. I still want to go to Africa."

Mom had a sister who was a nun, and Dad had a brother priest, so a religious vocation was looked upon as a blessing in the family. Mom and Dad, all smiles, said, "Okay, if you still want to leave, we won't stop you."

Sr. Sigmund (Martha), Sr. Angelina (Mom's sister)

Ever since grade school I had wanted to be a nun and work with the people in Africa. The idea to become a nun was not new to the family because I had wanted to leave for the convent after the eighth grade. My desire to work in Africa was my dream. My research stated that Africa is the world's second largest continent. More than three times the size of the U.S., it is home to enormous mountains, tropical rainforests, grassy savannas, three large deserts, and the world's longest river.

I had to choose which religious order to join, so I researched many religious organizations and found one that sent their missionaries only to Africa. I chose to go to Africa and only to Africa. The Missionary Sisters "White Sisters" of Our Lady of Africa was an order of nuns who worked only in Africa. I mailed a letter to them, telling them of my desire to become a nun and to work only in Africa. My dream was beginning to take the initial step after I received their acceptance letter.

Chapter 2

Franklin, Pennsylvania, 1958

The plan to become a nun had been in the inner part of my soul for a long time, so boys were not my main objective, although I was often told I was boy crazy. I corresponded with the Missionary Sisters of Our Lady of Africa, the order I wanted to join, and was given much information about the order and its founder. A few months later, they sent me an acceptance letter.

Preparations were now under way to head to Franklin, Pennsylvania, to begin my postulancy (initial training).

I think it was more difficult for my parents to see me leave then it was for me to take this first step. It was going to be the last time I would see them because this particular order of nuns did not allow their sisters to return home. It was a life-long commitment. Somehow, I didn't dwell on that part but was anxious to begin a new life. After a tearful goodbye to my family, I boarded the train and headed for Franklin to join the Missionary Sisters of Our Lady of Africa to work in an unknown continent where many new experiences awaited me.

According to the history of this order, in 1861 eight young Frenchwomen set foot on African soil in response to a call from the Archbishop of Algiers, Charles Cardinal Lavigerie, for women to work with the women of Africa. That was the beginning of the Missionary Sisters of Our Lady of Africa. Beginnings are always painful and getting this order of missionary nuns launched in the United States had been no exception. Long before any attempt was made to establish a convent in this country, a few young American girls heard about the sisters, decided to join them, and went to Canada for their early training.

I had never taken a train trip by myself before and found it to be long and lonely. After a long, two-day trip, I stopped in Chicago, where I was met by a family friend who took me to her house to stay the night. She made sure I was put on the right train in the morning. I wondered what kind of people I would meet and whether they would accept me into this order. As a young girl of eighteen, I soon found out, as I arrived in Franklin to begin my postulancy. I was met at the door by a sister dressed in a white robe and white veil. A cross hung around her neck with a red cord. A long, bone-colored rosary was attached to her side.

"Welcome, Martha, we've been waiting for you." I began to feel at ease. She took me to meet the other postulants. To make a good impression, I had worn my red high heels and beautiful white dress, but in this environment, they were hardly noticed. In another room, I put on a black dress with a white collar and black "old lady" shoes. This new attire made me feel strange, and I wondered if I would ever see my beautiful red high heels again. I was beginning a different kind of life, one completely foreign to me. My training began as part of a group of fourteen young women, consisting of Canadians and Americans.

The house, with a huge rock block exterior, priceless wooden banisters winding around the staircase, and spotless oak floors seemed to be extravagant. It didn't take me long to find this was far from the outward expression of truth. It took my breath away to see such luxury toned down to fit into the poverty-professed sisters' lifestyle.

Postulants in Franklin, Pennsylvania. Martha
(second row from top, first on left side

Beds were lined up in a large room separated by white curtains. Each of us had a cubicle. The cubicle was accessorized with a bed and a pillow filled with straw. Straw! I didn't expect something like this and had never before slept on a straw mattress. I always thought straw was used in a barn to feed cattle. The pungent smell of the straw with its unforgiving stalks poked my back. Uncomfortable is not quite the word to describe this unpleasant experience. I must admit it took me a long time to burrow a hole in the straw so I could sleep. The smell seemed to linger regardless of how well I washed. We were all in the same boat, so the smell of straw was everywhere. A nightstand beside the bed housed essentials such as toothpaste, hairbrush, comb, and small items. A "fichu" or a three-edged scarf had to be worn at night to cover our short hair. Mine usually came off, and I didn't make much effort to keep it on. I couldn't understand the meaning of this strange custom but was told it was a sign of humility to cover hair. A woman's hair was a sign of vanity, according to the sisters. I had never thought or been told a woman's hair was a sign of vanity. No one saw us anyway after dark.

Another custom I had to learn was the morning ritual. There was no "good morning" but a respectful silence because the "Grand Silence" began after evening prayers and lasted until after breakfast. The sisters in their white robes and the postulants in their black dresses with white collars walked in silence to the refectory (dining hall) for breakfast. All of us took a place around the long table and, after a prayer, sat down. The room was bare except for a few pictures and a cross. Since it was downstairs, there wasn't much light. For each meal, the postulants took turns reading from *Lives of the Saints*. Breakfast consisted of a meager bowl of coffee already mixed with milk, some kind of creamed cheese, which was awful, and some bread. When this creamed cheese first came on the table, I thought it was cottage cheese, so I took a generous helping. The first bite of this stuff forced me to grimace. To my utter dismay, it was not cottage cheese, but I had to force myself to eat it. I never found out what it was, but I noticed some of the other postulants had a difficult time eating it as well. I didn't repeat that experience. After this distasteful breakfast in silence, we headed back to the chapel for prayers and meditation.

The value of silence was taught and felt throughout the day. Prayer became the center of our daily routine. After prayers, we met together to discuss the daily work schedules. Sometimes I was assigned to work in the garden, other times to clean various rooms or go to the sewing room to sew clothes.

Kneeling was extremely difficult because we did so much of it on bare wood. My knees seem to hurt every time I knelt for prayer. They must have been weakened by all the kneeling. Padded kneelers were not to be seen in this house of hidden luxury. Kneeling on the wooden kneelers was not easy for me because my knees hurt so much and so often, yet I made the effort to kneel and didn't say anything. I suppose my knee problems, which continued through the years, probably began at this time. Another thing I had to learn was to sit up straight and not touch the back of the chair or bench. Since our backs could not touch the back of the bench or chair, knees hurt and backs ached.

TRAINING TO BE A NUN

Classes, during the day, consisted of learning the Bible, *Lives of the Saints*, the purpose of our life, and prayer. I had never questioned much in my life because it was a normal life with siblings and parents with no drastic changes. Spending so much time learning about the lives of the saints or our founder elicited questions I had never had before. What made me come here to this place? Why was I so determined to become a nun and go to Africa? Why would anyone want to give up the pleasures of the world? Who was I to try to fit into this austere way of life? And it was austere. Straw mattresses and straw-filled pillows, simple food, and little freedom. There were no luxuries, just a very simple lifestyle of work and prayer. It was only during my times of meditation and prayer that I felt most of these questions were answered. I really believed God had chosen me to eventually work with his people in Africa.

Work outside in the gardens in these black dresses, habits, as they were called, made work twice as difficult. Trying to dig in dirt with a long dress was impractical. I was always getting part of the skirt on the shovel. All this was done in silence, so I muttered to myself a lot.

Learning French was a necessity since the order was founded by a Frenchman, and most of the European sisters already spoke French. I didn't find learning French easy, but I tried. The French classes were some of the ones I dreaded. I enjoyed the singing lessons because I enjoyed music in whatever form. The Mother Superior had a beautiful voice and knew so many songs, which she taught us.

After lunch we played volleyball. This was a time when we talked as much as we wanted, and then it was back to class. We had to follow a rule that never allowed two of us to be together. This was known as a "particular friendship." Two sisters might become friends, so the "three rule" had to be observed. Confiding in two people was much more difficult than confiding in one person.

The location was breathtaking with the huge, old, rock house situated in a wooded area surrounded by mature trees. A walk in the back yard afforded a private time to enjoy the flowers, the birds, chipmunks, and squirrels, while making the Way of the Cross in complete seclusion. Each Station of the Cross was placed on a tree along the numerous bushes and trees that led to a forest-like section. These times of enjoying nature were a gift. I loved to watch the bluebirds, the finches, the robins, the doves, and ravens fly around and perch on the tree branches. Their freedom was like a breath of fresh air. The air was permeated with the scent of pine needles. The squirrels scampered around searching for food. The little chipmunks were so cute running after each other. In the wintertime, deer searched for food so close around the house.

In the summer evenings, we prayed and sang our goodnight outside on the front porch. One evening, as we sang, a whippoorwill in all his glory, joined in with his musical whippoorwill song. He whippoorwilled during a pause at an opportune moment. Since no talking was allowed because the grand silence had begun, the laughter wanting to bubble out of me was forced to stay inside. That whippoorwill will never know how much I enjoyed his contribution.

Living with the same people for months forged a bond between us, and we became friends. Most of us talked about our families and, in time, we knew how much this training meant to each of us. We became a family, striving for the same goals. Different assignments would be given to all of us, and we would probably end up in some country in Africa. We hoped we would meet again, either in Africa or in the United States. All of us had the same desire to work in Africa. Because life was so austere and challenging, some of my companions left during the following months. They just disappeared during the night, never to be seen again. No explanation given. No goodbyes said. This type of separation was difficult to understand because there was no contact with them again. It was hard to comprehend why one of the group left without a word and with no reason given. We were left to wonder why, what happened, and whether they would be all right. It seemed so unfair for those left behind. The ones who left were missed, and yet we couldn't talk about them.

Those first months I learned what homesickness and loneliness were. I hid many tears at times because, even though I was in a group, I was not of the group. I had never known life so austere with no one to share my feelings. Personal feelings were never brought up. I often thought of the good times I had with my family and the fun I had with Mary and Minny. We always talked a lot and knew how each other felt, but here in this environment, people lived together but still remained very far apart. In time, I guess I grew up or got used to the place and customs and began to look forward to my goal to become a nun.

Six months were long, but at the end of the six months, we were ready to begin our novitiate, which meant we had to move to Belleville, Illinois.

If I thought these six months were long and difficult, the next eighteen months proved to be another challenge. The novitiate was the serious time of prayer and contemplation in preparation for taking first vows of poverty, chastity, and obedience. We packed what little we had in the two cars and left for Belleville. I must admit silence was broken several times on the trip to Belleville.

Novitiate Training

Upon our arrival, a French Mother Superior greeted the newcomers with, "Welcome, sisters." The Mother Superior showed us around the house. We again had cubicles but no straw mattresses. We now became novices. Life changed drastically and at times was miserable because this disciplined French woman thought we Americans needed extra discipline. For any infraction, we did penance by eating a meal on our knees or having to kiss the floor. An infraction would consist of breaking silence and talking to someone or talking after the grand silence began. I spent many hours on my knees and kissed the floor more times than I care to remember. Humility was supposed to make us strong, and we were given many lessons and opportunities to learn. I wonder today if those so-called acts of humility were really effective.

Because of the eventual vow of poverty, we didn't have many clothes. One change of clothes, the woolen dress we had to wear in one hundred degree weather didn't improve our spirits much. Perspiration was a constant companion. The house did not have air conditioning, so it was hot all the time. I tended to perspire frequently because the heat bothered me. The wimple, the cloth around my head to keep my veil pinned to, was always wet. The heat and humidity made it so uncomfortable, drawing energy from the tasks at hand.

Did all this hardship make me stronger? I suppose, but I didn't realize it then.

Laundry was done once a week, so a change of clothes was eagerly anticipated. In the wintertime, the house bared its frosty breath of cold air. The radiators controlled the heat, so rooms were cold.

Eighteen months of classes, prayer, and meditation dragged by, but finally the day came to pronounce our vows of poverty, chastity, and obedience before the Bishop. My family traveled from Colorado Springs for this event. It had been a long two years since my departure. To see family members meant familiar faces, the sense of belonging, and the life-long bond renewed. Their visit was so short, but it did me a world of good. I knew it was a hardship on my parents to make the trip because they had little money to spare, but I appreciated it so much and loved seeing them. They will never know just how much it meant to me.

First Vows Ceremony

The ceremony took place in the church with the bishop. One by one we novices walked down the aisle in our wedding dresses. We were to become brides of Christ. During the ceremony, the Mother Superior handed us our white habits and veils, and we then processed out of the church. In one of the small rooms, the wedding dress was taken off. When all of us were dressed in our new robes, we processed down the aisle in our new white habits and white veils. Each of us stood before the bishop and pronounced the vows of poverty, chastity, and obedience. At this time, my name was changed to Sr. Sigmund because I took my father's name. The Mother Superior put the cross with the red cord around my neck, and a long rosary was placed at my side. We became Missionary Sisters of Our Lady of Africa, also known as "White Sisters" because of our white habits. This was another step to my final goal.

Sr. Sigmund (Martha)

After the First Vows ceremony, I was assigned to Washington, D.C., to attend college. This house was mainly a house of study. Another sister and I attended Immaculata College and, after meeting the required hours of study and work, obtained our associate degrees. I soon learned that studying in an academic environment is a lot different from studying in the convent. There were exams, which had to be passed, and a lot of homework. The two years passed, and the two of us received our degrees.

In the early 1960s in Washington, D.C., sing-alongs were popular. This type of gathering had a strange name, but it brought people out to parks. I was among the group of sisters who liked to sing, and after enduring long hours of practice to learn some African songs taught by a sister who had been in Africa for many years, I joined in the sing-alongs. This sister had been my Mother Superior in Franklin, Pennsylvania, a few years prior to this.

THE ED SULLIVAN SHOW

When the opportunity came to sing on the *Ed Sullivan Show*, I was chosen, along with nine other sisters, to board a bus headed for New York. It was during Holy Week just before Easter. With the American Mother Superior leading the choir, life was a lot easier. We did keep our times of silence on the bus ride, but our eyes didn't miss anything along the way. While sitting in the waiting room on Easter Sunday to go on stage with Ed Sullivan, the children who sang in the movie, *The Sound of Music*, were in the next room, so we had the chance to meet them.

"Hello, how are you? Are you excited to be on this show?" we asked.

"Oh, yes, we've been practicing a long time," they replied.

It was striking to see how mature these children were. Somehow they had lost their childlike innocence and had attained a mature attitude and demeanor. Parents accompanied the children, but they didn't seem to need them.

The moment came for Ed Sullivan to introduce us. I had written my family about this show, and I'm sure they spread the word that their daughter was going to appear on *The Ed Sullivan Show*. When introduced by Ed Sullivan, we put our best feet in our black nun shoes forward and sang an African song with the accompaniment of tambourines, an African drum, and gourd shakers. Our moment of fame lasted a few precious minutes. The unforgettable moment was short but never to be forgotten. The cameraman chose to get a close-up photo of me, so I treasure that photo today.

The rush and bustle of the stage hands depicted New York. The excitement to be on the same stage as Ed Sullivan was one of the highlights of my life. While in New York, we stood in a recording studio, surrounded by microphones and sang African songs and cut a record entitled *Suzanna*. The record didn't sell very well because this type of music was not popular in the United States at the time. Today, I still treasure the record with the picture of the "White Sister" playing the drum on the cover. She was my companion in college who later died in Africa from malaria.

The camera snaps it
and it's ours to keep . . .
that unbelievable moment
when eighteen missionary sisters
were TV stars.

The needle cuts it
and it's yours to keep . . .
that delightful moment in sound
when the rhythm of Africa's music
met the enterprise of American
nuns and SUZANNA was born!

Seriously, though,

SUZANNA is a rare collection of
moods and rhythms in African music
gathered by the White Sisters
over a period of fifty years in
mission posts throughout Africa.

Sister M. Sigmund, a member of the White Sisters of Africa and the daughter of Mr. and Mrs. Sigmund Leiker of 2429 N. Cascade, was featured on Ed Sullivan's television program Easter Sunday. She is the former Martha E. Leiker, a graduate of St. Mary's High School and an accomplished musician. In high school, she played the saxophone and bassoon for the school's band and orchestra. She entered the White Sisters' congregation in 1958 and is a member of the singing group which has been singing African Masses and other African music for a number of years. Recently they made a record which attracted Ed Sullivan's attention and led to the group's being invited to appear on his show.

RECORD COLLECTORS

Here's a real item for you. Africa's rich musical heritage in an album of traditional and Christian music.

side 1   folk songs from Congo, Uganda and Kabylia.

side 2   African mass songs and hymns from Rwanda, Congo, Tanzania and Uganda.

Please send me the new Aardvark l.p. album, "SUZANNA" recorded by the White Sisters.

Name _____

Address _____

Price of album (including a flyer with background information, African lyrics and English translations) is $4.50. A stereophonic cut (for stereo machines only) is available for $5.00.

regular ($4.50) ○   stereo ($5.00) ○
(please check which you prefer)

mail to: WHITE SISTERS' RECORD
RIVER ROAD
NEW BRUNSWICK, N.J. 08___

White Sisters recording record *Suzanna* Bottom photo caption: Martha

Missionary Sisters of Our Lady of Africa, Washington,
D.C. Martha (top row, fourth from left)

While in D.C., opportunities abounded to sing at common sing-along gatherings. Radio shows were also popular, and when asked to appear on the *Don McNeill Radio Show*, a few of us headed for his show. Our songs were heard on the air waves. This was not a normal thing for sisters to do, but it gave us the opportunity to meet people and tell them about our Order and what kind of work we did. Singing at different functions offered the opportunity to work together, sing together, and pray together.

Sisters on the *Don McNeill Radio Show*. Martha (second from right)

It was soon time to leave for England for further studies, so continuing my education to get a four-year degree was not considered, due to the demand for more sisters in Africa. I really wanted to get a four-year degree, but my superiors had other plans. They weren't my plans, and I wasn't too happy about them. Disappointment was an understatement, but my vow of obedience came into play, and I had to comply. I was learning what this vow of obedience really meant.

LONDON, ENGLAND

My time in D.C. was coming to a close, and with renewed excitement and anticipation, I headed to London for further studies. Preparing to fly off to London made me realize another step was being taken to bring my dream to fruition. I had never traveled out of the United States by myself, but now I was heading for a foreign country. The sisters in London lived in Kensington Park. Many nationalities lived under this one roof, and this changed views and outlooks for all of us. Listening to others and how they felt or presented themselves proved to be an education in itself.

"Since you are from Germany, what was your life like?" I asked.

"We went through war and know what it's like to have family members killed while serving their country," a sister responded.

Tensions between certain nationalities were keenly felt. I learned this fact because of the wars between certain countries in Europe. The lasting effect of these wars trickled down many generations, as evidenced in these young sisters.

The European sisters knew many languages because of the geographical areas in which they lived. By necessity, they had to learn other languages. They could so easily change from one language to another. Attitudes and viewpoints exhibited themselves during lively discussions. I had to make an effort to get used to the "new" English I heard everyday and ended up imitating it. When one hears a word many times, it soon becomes one's own. The word "lorry" for truck sounded unusual to me. Time was always half past one rather than one-thirty. The t's were pronounced and not garbled as in the United States. The British enunciate so well. It was a delight to listen to them, and this prompted me to closely watch my own pronunciation.

Living in London was a manifestation as to how different people were, but with effort and patience, we shared life together. We had a common bond, one that was shared by all.

A group of sisters took the underground (subway) to a college where more theological courses were taken.

"Is everyone ready to walk to the underground?" someone asked.

A group of young women dressed in white dresses with white veils getting on the train together and sitting together must have looked rather comical to the other passengers on the train. There were few conversations going on during the train ride, and we soon learned this to be one of the English customs. The silence was deafening.

Some days some of us took a walk, and on our walks, we saw gardens or flower boxes on the windows of "flats" (apartments). The gardens, an array of sweet williams, white freesia, blue lysianthus, kiwi roses, blue delphiniums, purple irises, and softer pastels and roses completed the miniature meadow. The aroma of the flowers made the world a brighter one. The British love and take such good care of their gardens.

On several occasion on my walks, I encountered some pets in trams (buggies). Pets were highly thought of and treated well. It wasn't uncommon to see a Pekingese with pink ribbons and bows on its head or tied to its ears being pushed around in a tram. Sometimes it was a miniature poodle, but it was a dog well cared for.

I walked down the famous Portobello Road open-air market. Visitors in their country's finest attire walked the same road and purchased antiques and artifacts and took advantage of bargains. There were other times when I had the opportunity to visit some of the castles. I was living in a fairytale country of castles. Walking through a castle was like reliving the past history of England, which is famous for its many castles in the surrounding countryside.

When the year of study ended, I was twenty-six years old. I received my assignment to Kabunda, Zambia—at last I was on my way to Africa.

Chapter 3

At the London Heathrow Airport, I boarded a plane to take this trip alone into an unknown world. Every time I changed planes, the plane became smaller and smaller. There was no direct route to Zambia. Smells became more acute. On the last small plane, looking out the window, I groaned to see such sparse vegetation. A few scrawny trees and bushes lined the dirt roads weaving their web around the parched land.

The plane touched the dehydrated soil in Mansa, Zambia. I walked slowly into the miniature terminal building resembling a hut. I looked around and found a French sister waiting for me.

"*Bon jour, Ma Soeur, Bienvenu,*" she said.

"Hello, Sister, how are you?" I replied.

"Did you have a good trip?" she asked.

"Yes, but it was long, and I had to change planes several times."

"We have a few miles to go, so when we collect your luggage, we'll be off."

I thought, *oh, great. Why did I want to come to Africa? Where is the beauty of this land of my dreams?* The airport was a very small building. When we walked outside, I saw only a few black faces. There wasn't much to see besides the airport and small runway. The dirt roads around the airport were dry and dusty. Only a small part of the runway was tarred for the small plane to land. Men in their brown shorts and women in their long wrap-around dresses walked on the dirt road.

The reality of its starkness hit hard. I found it difficult to speak and wanted to get back on the plane and head for home. My feet seemed to have forgotten they were supposed to move.

Disbelief and utter desolation overwhelmed me. I was now on African soil, not happy but disconcerted. My questions were many. My heart eluded me. Why did I want to come to such a barren, dry land? This was not what I had imagined as a teenager. What did I imagine? With mixed feelings, I was thankful to set foot on African soil but sad at the same time because I knew I would never see my family again. This was a life-long commitment. I had not dwelt on this aspect before, but a rule of this particular religious Order was that we could not return to our home country. Fortunately, this rule changed years later, which made it possible for me to return home after every four years.

The heat was stifling, but I climbed into the sister's white Volkswagen for a six-mile ride into the bush. At this point, I was ready to board the plane and forget this venture but couldn't. The dry soil cried for moisture. The bushes, stunted in their growth, belied harsh times. Dust was plentiful on peoples' clothes and hair. Where were the trees? I had always read trees were plentiful. Perhaps I missed in what area. There was nothing but scrubby brush. Was there no water or river nearby? This reality shot through my heart like a bolt of lightning. I didn't speak much on the road to Kabunda because I tried to calm down and see the landscape as it was. My home town in Kansas was dry but never like this. Everything appeared like it was just existing but not really alive. I saw no animals, no birds, not even insects.

When the VW "bug" finally stopped in front of a small house, a school and its play area enclosed the circle of dehydrated habitation. A French Mother Superior and a Canadian sister met me at the door. The Canadian sister was the headmistress of the middle school.

"Welcome, Sister Sigmund. We're so glad you finally made it. Come in and have something to drink."

Did I really want to take a chance and drink something? After the initial conversation, the sisters showed me a room that would be mine. I thought, *at least I'll have some privacy.*

The next morning I was awakened in the dark and walked in silence with the other two sisters a half mile down the dirt road to the church to attend Mass with the villagers. The church was a building that could have been built in the United States. Someone must have been a good architect in designing the building. How many people did it take to put each brick on top of brick to build a tall building like this? It was like walking into a European church until I entered and was struck by the stench. Nausea welled up. I was almost physically sick with the smell. I don't know why I looked up toward the ceiling and, to my horror, saw numerous bats hanging upside down from the rafters. It was so dark that, at first, I didn't see the droppings on the floor. The bats hung onto the rafters watching us with their beady eyes. I didn't recall stench like this from my early life on the farm. The other sisters walked past as if nothing was amiss, so I followed. A hurricane lamp was placed on the altar so we could see the priest, but since it was a black priest, his colorful vestments were all that were visible. Benches were nowhere to be found, only rows of six-inch cement slabs to kneel on with the one behind to sit on. It took some adjusting to sit on a small, cement slab.

Kneeling was unbelievably difficult and painful. My knees had experienced much pain before in Franklin, Pennsylvania, and in Belleville, Illinois, with kneeling on bare wood kneelers, but now another challenge had to be faced. African men sat on one side of the church, and the women on the other. There was no mixing the sexes. During the Mass, people raised their voices in a harmony never heard before by my ears. Hands clapped and bodies swayed to the music. The music was so melodious that my feet started tapping as well, and I started humming. The songs were so repetitious that it didn't take long to learn the verses in Cibemba. The music was wonderful, and participation was certainly not lacking here. Seeing women with babies sucking at the breast was not something I was used to seeing in church. It was a bit disconcerting at first, but it happened so often and seemed to be a common way for the women to feed their children, no matter where they were. Here it was a natural way of life.

LEARNING THE AFRICAN CULTURE AND LANGUAGE

My raison d'etre to be in Kabunda was to learn the Cibemba language. It was not a written language; therefore, there were no textbooks or grammar books. I made every effort to learn the language and the gestures of respect by listening to the villagers. Every day the French Mother Superior and I walked to the villages, where I listened to conversations and learned by osmosis. I learned the greeting "Mwapoleni, mukwai. Muli shani?" which means "Hello, how are you?" The villagers had little contact with the outside world, so seeing two white people dressed in white dresses was an enigma as well as a delight for them. Their world consisted of the next neighboring village or river.

I learned to ride a small motorbike, which took a bit of practice, but eventually I got used to it and rode to the different villages for my daily language lesson. Whenever I rode into the villages on my motorbike, the children came running alongside with their smiling faces screaming, "Ba Mama! Ba Mama!"

Martha on motorbike

This was their name for a religious sister. By the time I dodged the chickens and dogs, stopped, and got off my motorbike, a crowd of children surrounded me. The children made it so easy to learn to speak the language because they were so eager to help. As I pushed my motorbike and walked with them, the adults knew I was coming.

"Mwapoleni, mukwai. Muli shani?"

The men and women came out of their huts to greet me. Greetings were very important, and it always took time to find out how a family was doing. I would then sit down and try my best Cibemba on them. Sometimes with broad smiles and a twinkle in their eyes, they tipped me off that I had said the wrong thing, but I didn't know what it was. They were very kind and forgiving.

During the six months I spent in Kabunda, I visited the villages almost every day to hear the language and try conversing with the people. It wasn't an easy task, but I found it easier and easier to communicate with them.

While in Kabunda, during the last month, I fell ill, turning my favorite color, yellow. Yellow eyes, yellow skin, and lack of energy made me realize something was wrong. I didn't know what was wrong with me but knew something drastic was happening. It was difficult to get up in the morning and walk that half mile down to church. Sometimes I couldn't make it, so I stayed at home while the sisters left for Mass. Since malaria was common in the area, they gave me malaria pills, and for the first time, I experienced double vision. Seeing double slowed me down even more. Since I was seeing six sisters instead of three, they stopped giving me malaria pills, which cleared up that problem, but I was still not feeling right.

Surprises always arrive when not expected. It was during this time I received my next assignment to Ipusukilo, a mission where I was to teach married women in a home craft center in the Cibemba language. As ill as I was, I prepared my things to leave for this mission. The French sister who had met me at the airport was my chauffeur again on the dirt roads to Ipusukilo. Little did I know that the drinking water was the cause of these problems. Boiling water for the required length of time was not important to our cook, so, often, unsafe water was drunk.

IPUSUKILO, ZAMBIA, 1967

Sometime during the reign of Pope John XXIII, religious sisters could revert back to their baptismal names, so I had become Sister Martha. When I arrived in Ipusukilo, a community of three sisters greeted me warmly, "Welcome, Sr. Martha. We're so glad you came here."

Two of them were Canadian, of whom one was a nurse and the other, Mother Superior. The third sister was a German sister in charge of the home craft center. The Canadian nurse was in charge of the small hospital, which had no doctor. The house was built as any house in America and provided each of us our own bedroom.

A daily routine began in this new dry environment, and I soon found out the various schedules of the sisters. Once a week the laundry was done out in the small building five hundred yards from the main building, which housed a laundry room. A drum filled with water was built up on a frame, and firewood burned under the drum to heat the water. Pipes carrying water into the laundry room led to the cement sinks where water flowed into them. On those days we had hot water in the main house; otherwise, the water was cold all the time. There was a shower but no bath tub. I used the hot plate in the kitchen to heat pans of water, which made it possible to have a hot sponge bath. This was just another type of sacrifice, but it wasn't easy to give up a hot bath or shower. I guess I missed hot water so much that, today, I like my hot showers.

In the surroundings and in the back yard the orange, papaya, apple, and mango trees supplied us with an abundance of fruit. There was so much fruit, more than we could eat, so a lot of this fruit was given to the villagers, who appreciated the fruit by giving in return an egg or chicken. I often wondered why more fruit trees weren't planted in the villages.

The German sister in charge of the home craft center needed another teacher. This was to be my next challenging assignment.

HOME CRAFT CENTER

The day began with the women in their brightly colored wraps, carrying their babies on their backs, and the two of us sisters, circling the flag pole and singing the Zambian national anthem.

A class of fifty married women stayed on the premises in small houses for three months learning the basics of cleaning, cooking, sewing, and taking care of their children. Even though I was still ill, I rode my motorbike from the sisters' house down the dirt road a half mile to the center where the women and children went through the motions of daily life. Mothers were outside washing their children in small red, green, or blue basins. Others were busy tending their outside fires, where cooking the meals took place.

"Good morning, ladies!" I shouted from my motorbike.

"Mwapoleni, Ba Mama," they replied. My yellow eyes and my attempts to teach in Cibemba elicited much sympathy as they came into the classroom. The women knew I was ill and tried in their own way to help me in the classroom.

"Please come in and take your seats. We have to get started."

They were wives of prominent African leaders who were at the center so they helped me find the appropriate words to be understood. At times, I used the wrong words and had the women sewing sleeves where the pant legs should have gone.

"Oh, no, I told you to sew the wrong part here. You will have to tear it out and put it here."

Most of the time laughter was heard because they knew I was trying. They were forgiving, so we learned to work together.

Women at the home craft center. Ipusukilo, Zambia. Martha in white dress

ARMY ANTS

Some days there were surprises. One day as I rode my motorbike down to the center and approached the buildings on the compound, a lot of women stood outside, with their children wrapped on their backs, shouting to look at the swarm of ants.

"Ba Mama," the women cried. "Don't go near."

I stopped my motorbike and got off. In horror and disbelief, I watched an army of ants climb up the wall of one house, move in through the windows of the house, and out the other side, devour what they could in every house in their way. According to the women, these were the dangerous ants, so we kept a safe distance. After consuming whatever they could find in the houses, the army of ants moved into the bush. As far as I could find out, these were the army ants, which were dangerous. They are hundreds of thousands of ants that hunt and move all in one group. When the ants finally passed through the houses, the women entered the houses as if nothing unusual had happened. For me it was a most unusual sight to see one side of a house completely covered with ants entering into the open window, devouring the insects along the way, and exiting a window on the other side of the house—another experience of daily life for these women, but for me, a surreal incident.

AMBULANCE DRIVER

When you're in a foreign country you never know what you'll be asked to do. In conjunction with my teaching job, I became the hospital ambulance driver. The villagers came to the hospital and a sister nurse took care of them. Other times, there were difficult cases that were sent to the hospital in Kasama, a distance of a hundred miles on corrugated roads.

On one hot summer day, the sister nurse asked me to transport a pregnant woman to the Kasama hospital, because she had difficulty in delivering.

"You men, put her in the truck first," I said.

They talked among themselves and then several men in their tan shorts and tee shirts lifted the pregnant woman crying out with pain into the back of the blue Toyota pick-up. The back frame was covered by a canvas covering, which protected from sun, wind, and rain. It was customary that family members travel with the patient, so many of her family members pulled themselves up into the back of the pickup and found a space wherever they could. I don't know how they managed to get so many people in with her.

It was the rainy season, and the monsoon rains meant mud, mud, and more mud and a lot of potholes. With the windshield wipers working furiously, my hands gripping the steering wheel, I put the truck in gear (it was a stick shift) and wondered what my Dad would say if he were to see me now. I drove the truck as gingerly as I could over the potholes on this one-lane road. I could not avoid the many potholes, and the screams from the back of the pickup were not easily drowned out by the rain pelting the truck, so I slowed down even more. When the six long miles ended and Luwingu finally came into view, I breathed a sigh of relief and decided to stop at the small African hospital before continuing on to Kasama. The men pulled the gurney out with the woman and carried her into the hospital. I waited outside the examining room while the doctor examined her.

The doctor stepped out of the examining room and said, "You can take the woman back to the mission. She'll be all right." I looked at him with big eyes and a big question mark. He said with his gleaming white smile, "You can take the woman back to the mission to deliver her baby. The child's position has changed."

I asked, "What would happen if I hit potholes on the return trip? Would the child's position change back again?"

He laughed and said, "No, go ahead and return to the mission. The woman will deliver without any problems."

All my senses seemed to fine tune my driving ability because I drove extra carefully on the return trip. The sister nurse was surprised to see us.

"What happened?" she asked.

"The doctor at the Luwingu hospital said the trip helped to change the baby's position so she could deliver."

With the nurse's help, a baby appeared a few minutes later with me at her side. Her proud mother thanked me with her happy eyes and a warm handshake and said, "Ba Mama, my baby will be named after you." The little girl is now known as "Marita." Many such instances happened with my frequent trips.

On another day as ambulance driver, I transported a man one hundred miles to the Kasama hospital with his family members crowded in the back of the pickup.

"This is going to be a rough trip," I told the patient, "because I have to maintain a certain speed to keep on the road. Otherwise, I'll be all over it."

He nodded and said, "Ba Mama, I trust you. Do what you have to do."

It was not an easy trip, and I'm sure the patient with his broken femur was in agony. On later trips to Kasama, I visited him whenever I could and always received the greeting, "Ba Mama, I'm so glad to see you, and thank you for bringing me here. I hope you come to take me back to the mission when I'm well."

Even though I made many trips to the hospital transporting patients, I had not gotten over my illness and was still feeling the effects of it with extreme fatigue, lack of appetite, and a general no good feeling. No one seemed to know what was making me so ill.

Through the grapevine, the sisters heard a British doctor intended to attend a craft fair in Luwingu, the next town. I pulled my unwilling body into the pickup and drove the six miles to Luwingu. Finding the only white face in the crowd wasn't difficult. I approached the doctor, told him my symptoms, and asked for advice.

"Take your sunglasses off so I can see your eyes," he said.

I squinted at him because the bright sun hurt my eyes.

"You have hepatitis and should be in bed."

"What should I be doing?"

"There isn't much you can do except rest." I didn't exactly know what hepatitis was nor did I know what to do about it. I had an illness that I thought would go away eventually.

"Thank you, Doctor," I said and left. Seeing a doctor was a luxury, especially seeing a European doctor. I made my way back to the pickup, and climbing into it accelerated my heartbeat. Driving to the house of the "White Fathers" was my next stop. The White Fathers had the same founder as we did, hence the name. I had frequented their place many times when taking patients to Kasama. They were my "break" place. The Fathers, a Canadian and a Belgian, welcomed me with, "Hello, Sister. It's good to see you again. How are you doing?"

"I'm not too well and would like to rest before heading back to the mission." They gave me a bedroom, where I rested for a few hours before heading back home. When I got back to the mission, I talked to the sister nurse and asked her what I should do.

"Now that we know what your illness is, you need to rest because there isn't much else we can do for you."

I had my daily classes to teach, so during the day, I didn't get much chance to rest but did get a good long siesta after lunch. I soon realized that this was not going to go away by itself. I don't think I really knew the need for rest was so important and the danger was great. I rested whenever I could but probably not enough.

The month of August 1967 was a very important month. It was time to make my final vows with six other sisters scattered throughout Zambia and Malawi. The plan was to meet in Lilongwe, Malawi, a thousand mile trip from my present mission.

LUSAKA, ZAMBIA

Because of my health situation, the sisters didn't want me to make the trip, but I was determined. What exacerbated the situation was the fact that the first five hundred miles were on corrugated roads to Lusaka, where I was to meet another sister. There were no other drivers. After saying fond farewells to the sisters, I got into the small VW that was provided for the trip and departed. The journey was long on dirt roads, and dust was everywhere. The car didn't have air conditioning, so windows were left open. Sometimes it was suffocating. Another sister accompanied me but did not know how to drive. With sheer willpower and short breaks along the road, we reached Lusaka, exhausted but glad to have reached our destination safely.

That night, in my attempt to use the restroom, I woke up on the cold cement floor and wondered what I was doing on the floor. I tried to remember what I had been doing. I pulled myself up and kept my hand on the wall to find my way back to the bedroom. The bed had never felt so good. In the morning, I told the sister superior what had happened during the night, so I was told not to get up or try to go to Mass the next morning.

"Stay in bed and rest. You had a long trip. You're not well."

I'll always remember her kindness and understanding. It didn't take much more than that to remain where I was. My bed was my comfort that day. I slept most of the time.

Because the time was getting so close to the retreat and final vows ceremony in Malawi, I didn't have much chance to rest anymore. The following day, two of us sisters were on the road with a Canadian sister at the wheel en route to Lilongwe, Malawi. "Try to rest and I'll drive," she said. I gladly became the passenger.

LEPER COLONY

Along the way a leper colony was the next stop. We decided to stop because no one visited the colony, and the people were happy to see the sisters. As we drove near the camp, we saw the huts were scattered in uneven lines on the compound. Walking into the camp, the smell overwhelmed me because I wasn't feeling well anyway. I felt my stomach churning but forced the juices to stay where they were. I didn't think I could do such a thing, but my respect for such deformed people made it possible. Small children clung to their mothers unaware of their deformities. It was like walking back into Bible times of suffering. The leper stories from the Bible came vividly to mind. I was seeing the reality here in this camp. The smell of small, wood-burning fires for cooking was everywhere. Men and women with rags covering hand stumps, fingers missing, noses missing, feet missing, and other covered body parts missing, met us with their warm greeting, "Ba Mama. Welcome."

We asked, "How are you doing, and how are your children? Is there anything we can do for you?"

Smiles and grateful eyes were their response.

We walked around the camp giving as much encouragement as we could. Some of the people hobbled around with the aid of sticks or poles they had made from the tree trunks. Women tended their small fires, preparing meals, with their babies wrapped on their backs. Some of the children were picking up sticks to keep the fires going. They were all affected in some way, yet everyone, young or old, helped each other to survive. It was a colony of suffering, yet they clung to life, striving to live what quality of life they knew. Why were so much suffering, isolation, and pain corralled in such a small space? How was this colony started and by whom? The priests and nuns were the only visitors who came to this camp of suffering. I don't think a doctor who could help them ever came to this camp. They were too afraid of contracting the disease. These people didn't ask for this disease but just happened to be the ones to contract it. They had hopes and dreams like everyone else, and yet they were isolated into a camp with no outside contact with the world. I didn't even see a radio. The experience of meeting such maimed people was the most horrific sight I have ever seen, one that will forever be imbedded in my mind.

Lilongwe, Malawi, 1967

The leper colony was behind us but still very much on our minds as we continued our journey to Lilongwe, Malawi. The five hundred miles from Lusaka finally came to an end. Getting out of the car, the sisters greeted us. Startled by my appearance, weight loss, and pale complexion, the sisters immediately took me into the hospital that was on the premises. While I was in this state of low energy, I was still determined to make the trip to Bembeke to join the group to make the short retreat and pronounce our final vows. Due to this illness, that goal seemed to fade. By this time, I was very weak, and while in the hospital, contracted strep throat, which weakened my condition even more

It was during this time I didn't care if I lived or died. I really had no desire to go on. I was so sick and weak I didn't feel I would ever regain my strength. I had never reached this bottomless pit before. But as the days passed and with the gentle care of the sisters, little by little, I managed to get my strength back and voiced my desire to join my group in Bembeke, a small town a short distance away.

Final Vows Ceremony

The short trip to Bembeke was tiring, but I was glad to be with my companions. Seven of us were to take our vows together. Our Mother General, a German sister, had come all the way from Frascati, Italy, to attend the ceremony. My participation in the group retreat was non-existent. The priest came to my bedside to pray with me, but I was in no condition to play an active part. With the doctor's permission, I remained in bed until the ceremony and returned to bed rest after the ceremony was over. Two days later, the day finally came for the seven of us to make our final vows. Still determined, I struggled to get up and stand on my feet. Since I was the youngest in the group, I was the first to stand before the African Bishop and pronounce my final vows of poverty, chastity, and obedience. It was a very solemn moment. The other six sisters recited their vows one by one. We had now made a life-long commitment to follow God as religious sisters. I must admit most of the ceremony was a blur.

Final profession of vows in front of Bishop. Bembeke,
Malawi. Martha (last on the right)

After the ceremony, we enjoyed a wonderful meal and were happy that all of us had made a final commitment to the Lord. When the day ended, we said our farewells as the others sisters returned to their missions, and I was sent back to Lilongwe to rest.

Shortly after, because my visa to remain in Malawi was about to expire, the Regional Superior sent me to a small mission on the border of Zambia and Malawi to await my work permit to teach at the secondary school in Lilongwe. She decided to keep me in Malawi. I was not happy with this decision, but weak as I was and having just taken my final vow of obedience, I had no choice. My desire was to return to Zambia.

In 1966, Malawi became a republic, and Dr. Hastings Kamuzu Banda assumed the presidency.

LUMEZI, ZAMBIA, 1967

Lumezi, a small community of two sisters, one Dutch and one Canadian, invited me into their home for a month to rest. Life was slow and easy going. No one was ever in a hurry.

"Sister, we'll have to prepare some food to take to the patients today," one of them said.

"Yes, I've already put the pans on the stove," the other replied.

The two sisters took care of many of the patients in the hospital by taking food to them because the hospital did not provide the food. Families of some patients lived too far away to bring food, so the sisters did the job for them.

My time was spent in resting and praying. I was not asked to do any work or help at the hospital. I was truly given time to rest, which proved beneficial to me. Every day I rested as much as I could, but this was also a difficult time for me. I did not want to work in Malawi because my heart was in Zambia. I had made so much effort to learn their language and customs and found it difficult to understand why I had gone through so much in another country, when now I was asked to remain in a country other than what I wanted. I had grown to know and understand the Zambian people.

"Must I learn another language and customs to remain in Malawi?" A daily inner struggle raged to make the decision to remain in Malawi and teach in the secondary school. Many long days were spent in meditation and prayer to reach a point of resignation. When that point of resignation finally came and I was at peace with the decision, I was absolutely shocked to receive a letter from the Regional Superior telling me to return to Zambia. My world turned around. I realized that God does answer prayers. As soon as I could get my things together, the sisters drove me back to Lusaka, Zambia, to begin my new life as bursar (comptroller, accountant, and administrator all rolled into one) for the ten houses of sisters in Zambia.

Chapter 4

Lusaka, Zambia, 1967–1975

Lusaka, the capitol of Zambia, presented a variety of nationalities due to the numerous embassies housed in the capitol. It was a fascinating hub of activity with its varied sports, embassy receptions, meetings among the represented countries, open-air markets, imported food, and local food. It was a melting pot of countries.

In 1953, Northern Rhodesia became a member of the Federation of Rhodesia and Nyasaland, but the federation formally dissolved on December 31, 1963. On October 24, 1964, Northern Rhodesia became an independent republic, and its name was changed to Zambia. Kenneth Kaunda, the leader of the ruling United National Independence Party (UNIP) became the nation's first president.

The surrounding area consisted mostly of flat grassland, which supported ranches and farms. Termite mounds ten to twenty feet high were a regular feature of the landscape. Once again, I was in a country of diverse economic and environmental uncertainties. Welcomed by two Canadians and a German sister in Lusaka, I soon became familiar with the U-shaped house with each bedroom door leading to the inner courtyard. To get to the dining room, living room, and kitchen, each of us had to walk along the inner courtyard to the main house. The house was large to accommodate visiting sisters as they came through Lusaka en route to various missions. Each bedroom was small with just a small window, bed, and nightstand. A common bathroom was located at one of the corners of the inner courtyard, and another was located in the main house.

My title as bursar for the sisters' ten houses meant I had to prepare budgets for each house and collect the salaries of the sister teachers and nurses. I had to crisscross the country to visit each house since there were great distances to be covered. Because computers were still unknown, my manual typewriter got its daily workout. I typed letters and arranged visits to the various houses.

A blue Toyota station wagon, my constant companion on many long trips, became my means of transportation because the nearest sisters' house was a distance of four hundred miles, accessible only on dirt roads. The car was not air-conditioned, so my grey dress, which was worn on trips, acquired a red tinge due to the dust and dirt on the roads. Sneezing and coughing denoted the duet in my lungs. Few signs dotted the dirt roads to aid a traveler, so recognizing a clump of trees, a sign on a tree, or perhaps a spare tire left as a sign post by a tree or some other form of identification along the way made it possible to know where to turn off to one of the missions.

Martha on trip in Zambia

I also learned to use the "facilities of the bush" when needed but always looked around for snakes. There were no gas stations for a rest stop or use of facilities. Whenever I needed the use of the bush, I got out of the car and looked around to see if any villages were near, but usually, they were too far away. I made my way into the scrawny bushes, looked around for anything that might be crawling, and then squatted. Since I had to carry my own toilet paper, I did have some luxury.

Gerry cans of gas were always carried in my car to fill up when the gas gauge dipped low. When I had the misfortunate to have a flat tire, of necessity, I quickly learned how to change tires. There would be no one to help me on the road unless I waited for hours for someone to come by. It didn't take long to become quite independent and have the necessary supplies in the car.

One of the houses was situated on an island. I drove to the dock and boarded the small boat to cross the lake to Chilubi, a tiny split of land in the middle of Lake Banqweulu. The small motor boat took a little longer than I liked. Since I grew up in a landlocked state, I wasn't used to being around water. When we reached the other side of the lake, the sisters were there to greet me warmly, and the villagers broke into song, clapping their hands. It was a big event to have company on the island. The village kids greeted me with their big smiles and happy eyes.

There was one vehicle on the island, so the jeep that was used made a grand entry. We couldn't go very far because the island was small. After telling the sisters all the news and getting my business done with the Mother Superior, I was taken back to the dock and headed for the other side to get my car. The whole village came down to the dock to see me off. It was like a grand farewell.

Martha (driver) and another sister visiting a school on Chilubi Island

DEATH OF A VILLAGE CHIEF

During my travels, a village chief had died in one of the villages. Attending a funeral of this kind showed me another instance of how cultures are so different. As was the custom, the village chief's body was preserved for thirty days before burial. I walked into the dark hut, and as my eyes adjusted to the dark interior, was startled to see the chief sitting upright on a chair holding his staff in one hand. Women in their brightly colored wraps, wailed and kept a small fire burning, probably to mask the odor of decay. Somber men sat on the opposite side of the women. The smell instinctively made me want to cover my nose, but etiquette stopped me. I had attended other funerals where wailing women rolled on the ground, while the men lowered the body in the ground. Death in Africa is viewed as we view it in the United States. There is life, and there is death. In this land, women wail and sometimes roll on the ground while men look somber. The loss of a loved one affects all in different ways. Some grieve openly while others internalize the loss. But death affects all of us with sadness and pain regardless of race, color, or gender. The outward expression changes, depending on locale, and paying tribute is as widely different as the people around us.

ADDITIONAL DUTIES AS BURSAR

Another part of my job was to purchase cars, trucks, refrigerators, or any large item the missions needed and arrange for the transport to each particular mission. Dealing with car dealerships and the mounds of paper to read and sign to import a car challenged both the dealer and the buyer. For some of the requested items, I had to travel to another large town through fifty miles of the Congo to the other side of the Zambian border. The fifty miles resembled parts of uninhabited land with nothing visible except dirt, brush, and more dirt and dust. No villages were in sight because no lake or pond for needed water was near. There were two borders to cross, one leaving Zambia and a second entering the Congo side.

On my return trip, my car was loaded with purchases, which I always covered because the guards would come over to the blue Toyota and peer inside to see what purchases I had made. During one particular incident, I locked the car, got out, and walked into the customs hut to show my passport, which had my official name stamped in it. It was apparent I was a nun by my white dress and veil.

"Sister, can you take this man with you to the Zambian border?"

"No, I'm sorry. I can't," I replied.

"Sister, we need this man to be taken to the other border."

Again, I refused. The insistence to take someone frightened me because, in the car, I never knew what to expect. I could easily have disappeared in those fifty miles, and no one would ever know what happened. It would have been one of those unsolved mysteries.

During another incident, the guard insisted I take a man with me across the Congo to the eastern side of Zambia. I refused. After repeated requests, I still refused. His face showed a stoic sign of frustration, but he finally stamped my passport and let me go. I walked quickly to my car, heart pounding, got into the car, locked the doors, and with clenched hands on the steering wheel, waited for the barrier to be lifted. No guard came. What would I do if the customs guard insisted again? Would they let me continue my journey to the other side of Zambia? Time froze. Ten long minutes later, the guard came out of the hut, walked to the barrier, and lifted it. I waved a thank you and slammed hard on the accelerator. Those fifty miles through the Congo flew by that time.

I liked working with the sisters, traveling to the various houses to meet them and help them make life a little easier. Some of the time, it demanded more than what I expected, especially crossing borders.

GAME RESERVE

The White Fathers (they, too, wore white robes), had a house in Lusaka not far from ours. Since Zambia had huge game reserves on vast areas of land, a White Father invited another sister and me to accompany him into a game reserve. He loved taking pictures of animals and wanted to get as many photos of the animals in the reserve as he could. Sr. Beverly and I packed small bags, and off we went with Fr. George in his white Peugeot. We drove into the bush for miles and miles into the Luwangwa Valley until we approached a guardhouse. An armed guard with his rifle slung over his shoulder stopped the car and asked if we had the proper papers, which Fr. George had gotten. He instructed us to follow him.

"Follow me, and I will show you where the cabins are for visitors." He gunned up his jeep's motor, and we followed him for another hour until we came to a clearing where a few round huts stood. These huts were to be our sleeping quarters. Fr. George stopped the car, and we got out to unload our food and small suitcases. Sr. Beverly and I shared one hut while Fr. George had another. He was armed with all his camera equipment. The two of us sisters had taken some jeans and tops to wear, so we removed our veils for this time to be shared with the wild animals. We walked around the camp to see just what we needed to cook our meals. It was a campsite, so both Sr. Beverly and I went searching for small branches to feed a fire. Fr. George was unloading his camera equipment. That night we made our meal of hot dogs around the small fire. We now shared our space with wild animals.

Early the next morning, we climbed into the Land Rover with the armed guard to drive down to the river where the animals had to come to drink before starting their day of hunting. Driving over a rough, one-lane dirt road, we arrived at the water hole. Gazelles, water buffalo, wildebeests, hippos, elephants, and birds of all descriptions were drinking. Mesmerized by the activity of the animals, we stayed for a while watching them come and saunter off. The gazelles were alert all the time even though their noses dipped into the water. The elephants exhibited little fear as they moved around as they liked. Some majestic giraffes were off in the distance. Fr. George snapped, snapped, and snapped. I wondered how many rolls of film he had brought. As the sun began to show its strength, many of the animals left for shady places to rest or hunt. It was only during dusk or dawn that animals could be seen, so we headed back to the campsite with the guard. Back at the camp, we noticed some elephants down in the marsh. Taking advantage of every opportunity, Fr. George lugged his cameras and tripod and set them up to take pictures of the elephants with their young.

The elephants were in the marsh so no danger seemed to be imminent. They are protective of their young and don't like anyone around, especially humans. A mother elephant turned and began making her way towards us. Because she was knee deep in mud, she moved slowly.

"Martha, look at the young elephants. Aren't they cute?" Sr. Beverly asked.

"Yes, they really are, but they're so big for babies."

We continued to watch while Fr. George clicked away with his cameras. All of a sudden, when the mother elephant arrived on dry land, she came at us with such determination and speed, Fr George's cameras and tripod went flying. We ran for the cabins. I'm sure I let out a few screams, and so did Beverly. The guard saw what was happening and yelled at us to get inside the cabins.

From the cabin window, we could see the elephant's ears flapping up and down, her trunk pushed its way up and down the tree on the periphery of the camp, and her huge right foot was stomping angrily. The screeching was ear piercing. My heart pounded as loudly as the elephant screeched. Sr. Beverly didn't look too well, either. We both looked at each other and thanked the Lord we were safe. Who knew an elephant would come after us?

After all, we weren't bothering it. Apparently, the elephant thought we got too close to her young. I'm sure Fr. George's heart was thumping away, and he was probably wondering if the elephant stomped on his camera equipment.

"Father, are you all right?" I yelled to him.

"Yes, I'm okay."

The angry elephant remained there for thirty minutes and then slowly moved away. It took a while, but all of us calmed down. So much for taking pictures of elephants. After that incident we were more careful. Father walked to the spot where he had set up his cameras to find his camera equipment on the ground but not damaged.

The next day Fr. George decided he wanted to look for lions, so the three of us followed the armed guard and headed out to hunt for lions. Hunt for lions! Whoever heard of such a thing without weapons? I couldn't believe I was part of this crazy group. The armed guard headed the small detail of a priest and two nuns with me bringing up the rear. My thoughts were on a potential newspaper headline: "A Priest and Two Nuns Eaten by Lions."

Bringing up the rear didn't appeal to me because, with each step my fear grew stronger and stronger, so I inched my way up behind the guard. I thought I would at least have a chance if the lions attacked because the guard had a rifle. This safari continued on for a few hours, but I longed for it to be over. There was no way I could go back to the camp by myself, so caught in this trap, I had to continue. This was not my kind of enjoyment. Well, we didn't see any lions, but we heard their roars off in the distance. A lion's roar can be heard five miles away. I breathed a long sign of relief when we headed back to the camp. There was no chance I would ever do this again. Walking safaris to find lions was not something I wanted to repeat.

On the last day of our three-day trip, we climbed into the Land Rover again and drove around despite the heat. The guard stopped near some trees to watch giraffes when, to our utter surprise, on the side of the road next to us under a tree, I saw two lions taking their siesta. They looked like sleepy, overgrown cats and couldn't have been more than three hundred feet from our car. I hurriedly rolled up my window and whispered to the others.

"Look, over here, there are two lions under the tree."

Fr. George, sitting in the front seat with the guard, with his camera ready, clicked away and took many shots during that moment. Beverly, quietly and swiftly, moved as far as she could to the other side of the seat. I guess she wasn't too pleased about being so close to lions, either. When the lions started to move, the guard stepped on the accelerator, and we moved away from them. I thought we had had enough excitement to last a lifetime.

We left the camp and drove out of the game reserve and headed for Lusaka. I know both Beverly and I were relieved, but Fr. George had certainly enjoyed his stay. He had his photos developed and proudly enjoyed showing them to everyone.

THIRTY-DAY RETREAT

After so many years of religious profession, a sister must make a thirty-day retreat. My time to do this was coming, although I didn't look forward to it. The Regional Mother Superior had asked me to go to Italy and make this retreat some time ago, but I had refused. However, when the request came a second time, I knew I had to go. I was reassured I would return to Zambia and resume my job as Bursar, so I accepted and prepared to leave for Frascati, Italy, where the retreat was to be held at our Motherhouse.

FRASCATI, ITALY, 1975

After much inner struggle, I resigned myself to make the trip to Frascati for the thirty-day retreat. It had been a difficult decision, because it was not something I wanted to do. A long retreat was not to my liking, nor did I have any desire to pray and keep silence for so long. I was used to a lot of activity and being my "own boss." However, the evitable happens.

I packed a suitcase and flew to Italy to stay at our Motherhouse situated on a hill with a breathtaking view of the Italian city. I had never been in such a huge house before. In the morning, you could hear the church bells reverberate through the neighborhood. The retreat began with its inner soul searching for the twenty-five sisters. As the days dragged by, I spoke to the priest concerning some hesitations and doubts about my continuing as a nun. When I left Lusaka, the Regional Superior had promised I would return to my job as bursar, which I believed I did well. I felt comfortable in performing this service for the sisters.

The retreat continued, and almost two weeks later, to my surprise, I received a letter from the Regional Superior asking me, upon my return to Zambia, to transfer to the secondary school for girls in Chilubula to look after all the needs of the school and the girls. My disappointment was unspeakable because I had visited that mission many times and knew this was not the place for me. I felt stifled and knew that, if I accepted the position, I couldn't do a good job and would be unhappy. It wouldn't be fair either to the sisters and school girls or to me. There was only one way to resolve this dilemma.

I sent the Regional Superior a negative response and decided that it would be best for me to take a year's leave of absence. I felt the Regional Superior had gone back on her word. I suppose she felt the need was greater at the girls' school, but in my heart, I knew it was not the place for me. This event seemed to cement my decision to not return to Zambia. A year's leave of absence would give me another perspective. Perhaps it was the best for all of us.

At the end of the two weeks at the retreat, I decided to leave for the United

States. Again, as was the custom, I left in the middle of the night. I was sorry to leave because I wanted to tell some of my friends I had made the reason for my departure. I never got that opportunity. No one else knew I was leaving. This time, I was the one leaving the question mark for the others to surmise the reason for my departure. I will never know what they thought.

LEAVE OF ABSENCE, DENVER, COLORADO, 1975–1976

Returning to the States was not on my agenda, but here I was. The plane landed in Colorado Springs, where I spent time with my parents. I knew I couldn't stay with them for long because I had never grown up in their eyes. I was still their eighteen year old daughter. I'm sure I was a disappointment to them because no one in the family had ever left the religious life. I had this year to think about what I was doing and make a decision whether to return to the sisters or not.

My twin sister Mary lived in Denver, so I decided to stay with her for awhile until I found an apartment. Mary helped me get started because I had nothing in the way of dishes, pots and pans, or the basic necessities to set up an apartment. I had to face finding a job to support myself. I was thirty-five years old and had never before had to look for a job.

I wasn't sure what my qualifications were to find a job. However, I applied at a school district and became a department head secretary. After several months, the department downsized, and I went into a transcription pool. It was a good but boring experience, and I knew it wasn't for me, so I looked for something else.

I found another job as executive secretary to the president of a cement consulting company. This was probably the worst experience and biggest mistake I've ever made. The company president fired his staff on the spur of the moment for minor infractions. I witnessed his firing some of the men for small mistakes of no consequence. The atmosphere was tense. Most of his staff did not stay around long. I had never seen people treated in such a demeaning manner. It was not a happy place to work because of the tension and the fear the staff had of losing their jobs. After a few days, I knew this place was not a healthy environment for me.

After two weeks of this tense situation, on a warm, sunny fall day, I drove to downtown Denver and found a government building to get an application to apply for a government position. Whether it was for the state or federal government didn't matter to me. I picked up the application, but as I walked out the building, a poster displayed on the bulletin board caught my eye. Uncle Sam in his glory and big hat with the red, white and blue background, pointed his finger and said, "I Need YOU." In fine print, it stated that the

CIA needed people to work in the foreign service. I saw Africa listed and knew instantly that Africa was going to be my next destination. I had already been through the cultural shock having lived in several African countries. I knew I wouldn't be a flight risk for the government as some new recruits were. They quickly found out that they couldn't survive in Africa because life was too different, so they broke their contracts and came back stateside. The government lost a lot of money moving them back and forth. If I returned to Africa, I knew what to expect.

I must admit I didn't know what the CIA was or did. I had been out of the country for so many years and didn't follow American politics. As a nun in Africa, the only radio station blaring out news was the BBC, and little was said about the United States. The local radio station didn't broadcast much overseas news because it was censored.

Dance Class

In the meantime, while working in Denver, I decided I needed some social skills, so enrolled in the Arthur Murray Dance School. This type of socialization was completely out of my sphere of experience. I drove to this building in downtown Denver once a week to learn how to dance. I soon found out there were many people in the same boat as I who lacked social graces.

"Hold your head up this way," I was told. "Your hand goes like this." The instructor put my hand on his shoulder. "We're going to learn the two-step."

I stepped on his toes more than once, but I'm sure he was used to it and took it graciously. The lessons were grueling because I had to learn so many dance steps. As my skills progressed with much practicing, I was transferred to the next level. With time, it became a real treat to be on the dance floor, knowing what I was doing.

Years later, when I was in D.C., I finished my dancing course and was chosen to dance in a competition. My mother flew to D.C. to watch this competition. The dancers were out on the floor, and as each competition ended, my heart pounded because it was getting closer and closer to the final dance. My partner led me in a waltz, which I loved to do, and we moved in a rhythm to rival the other competitors. As the dance ended, my mother, with a big smile looked at me with approving eyes.

"You looked so nice out there dancing. You were so graceful." I won second place in the competition with hundreds of dancers trying their best in this beautiful ballroom setting.

My year's leave of absence was drawing to a close. It wasn't difficult to make the decision to leave the sisters' order because now I felt I had to follow Christ in a different way. I wrote my letter to the Pope asking to be released from my three vows of poverty, chastity, and obedience. This was a time in the Catholic Church when many religious nuns left their orders. A letter received later from the Holy Father did release me of the vows, so I could now follow another life direction. I was at peace with myself and ready to begin a new phase of my life. This new direction led me to a life of secrecy.

Pending Job with CIA

I mailed my application to the CIA, and it was answered by a phone call. I was asked to undergo a medical exam and an interview, so I flew to D.C. In the waiting room, my name was called, and I walked in for an interview. Then the background check began. It was amusing because I wondered what kind of background check could they do on me. I had been a nun for seventeen years. I didn't think I was any kind of threat.

During the following months, I received phone calls asking me if I was still interested. Each time I replied in the affirmative. After some months, an official letter from the CIA landed in my mailbox requesting my presence in Washington, D.C., on a certain date to begin work. Cloud nine was floating around, and I was on top of it. Africa, here I come again.

My next few weeks were occupied with cleaning the apartment, moving things, and packing. While I was preparing for the trip to Washington, D.C., my brother, Lee, convinced me that I should not drive the three thousand miles alone, so his wife, my sister-in-law, Kay, accompanied me on the trip. With the car loaded, we crossed one state after another, passing the snow-covered fields, which reminded me of the country's vastness. Some of the roads had ice patches along the way. The miles flew by. Three days later, we arrived in Virginia, so I took up residence in my new apartment. Kay flew back to Colorado Springs.

Chapter 5

CENTRAL INTELLIGENCE AGENCY, LANGLEY, VIRGINIA, 1978

The Central Intelligence Agency (CIA) is a civilian intelligence agency of the United States government. It's an independent agency responsible for providing national security intelligence to senior United States policymakers, and its primary function is collecting and analyzing information about foreign governments, corporations, and individuals, which it uses to advise public policymakers. The agency conducts covert operations and paramilitary actions and exerts foreign political influence.

I drove onto the compound of the CIA wondering what all the security was about. One of the guards told me to go into a room to get a badge and fill out some paperwork. The guard escorted me into the room where a lot of new people were waiting. While waiting to be called for an interview, I looked around and watched all the others who were also there waiting for a job. Some of them were young, and some around my age. Several hours passed and conversations began. Some of us older people (in our 30s) got together, so I met several ladies in the room who remain my friends today. I guess we formed a certain bond that day. After the interview, I was assigned to the travel section. I didn't know how the CIA worked but was pleased to have finally arrived in D.C. to begin this new job.

Outside, a snow storm raged and blew its mighty wind. Traffic came to a halt. At the end of the day, there was no way I could reach my apartment except to trudge knee deep in the snow for several blocks, which I did. It took me over an hour to reach my apartment. This was a most unwelcomed storm, not the welcome I expected to receive in the most important city in the United States.

One of the first things I had to do was to affirm my loyalty to the United States by taking an oath to serve the country. I began work in my department and soon learned about my duties. In the beginning, the duties seemed simple enough, but as time went on, the duties increased as well as the responsibility. Not only was I expected to do a job, but training was offered. I was sent to different buildings for different areas of training. I had mentioned to my supervisor many times that I had been in Africa and wanted to return.

It was due to his intervention that I was transferred to the Africa Division, where I began to understand the mission of the CIA from the "field" aspect. To my surprise, I was in a secret agency. Keeping secrets was nothing new to me, because I had learned to keep silence as a nun.

Upon arrival on the CIA grounds, I had to produce my badge for the guard to check my ID to get cleared for the drive to the west parking lot, where most people found a parking space. It was a good fifteen minute walk to the main building. With my fashionable suits, I wore heels that were not comfortable and hurt most of the time. Sneakers were not "in" at this time. Once inside the building, again, my badge had to be screened before entering the "inner sanctum."

Many times I had to walk to other offices in the building and found the hallways unending and a complete maze. Hallways seem to lead in every direction. I did manage to find one of the most important places, the cafeteria. Some offices were off-limits, and that piqued my curiosity.

I made friends at work easily, but, because of the different areas where people lived there wasn't much socializing after hours. It wasn't easy to find friends outside the office. I commuted sixteen miles to work each day, so living in a rural area made it even more difficult. I soon learned who my neighbors were and talked to them. Many people commuted from Maryland, Pennsylvania, Washington, D.C. proper, and Virginia. The year of intense training came to an end with an assignment to Africa.

AFRICA, 1978–1980

My bags were packed, and my household goods were already on the way to my new destination in Africa. A new leaf in my life was about to turn. In past years, I had traveled to Africa knowing I would be taken care of by the sisters, but this time it was different. I was on my own going to an African country where I knew no one and didn't know what to expect.

A friendly couple designated to look after the "newbie" met me at the airport. "Welcome, Martha, How was the trip?" they asked.

"It was long but I'm glad to be here."

They kept a close watch on my luggage because baggage disappeared while passengers milled around.

Many of the government personnel were housed in a two-story apartment building. Most of us were given a furnished, two-bedroom apartment, which

I also received. It was a very comfortable apartment, and I felt safe because there were other employees in this apartment building.

Basic food items were put in place until I had time to do my own shopping. My household goods had arrived, so I made arrangements to have them delivered to my new home. Parking was beneath the apartment building. Whenever I walked down to the lower level to get my car, rats twice the size of other rats I've seen ran along the pipes. They were something to be feared because of their sheer number and size. I hurried to the car fearful of those black, disgusting, long-tailed rodents ganging up on me.

The one elevator in the building didn't work very often, and light bulbs in the stairwell were not changed when burned out, so carrying a flashlight was a necessity. It wasn't always easy to carry bags of groceries in the dark and find my way up the stairs with a flashlight guiding the way.

The guards greeted me on my first day of work, checked over my identification to enter, and then escorted me to the office where I was to work. My boss, a Japanese American, another officer, and a secretary welcomed me as part of their team. I was escorted around the building to meet other officers. This whole experience was so different from my past experiences because I wasn't used to all the cipher locks, the safes, and the tight security. At the end of the day, everything had to be locked up with nothing left on desks. The guards, on their rounds, made sure nothing was left out; otherwise, a security violation was issued. The number of safe combinations and the cipher locks I had to remember to get through the building to my office was not for the faint of heart.

LOCAL MARKET

Stores in the town had imported expensive merchandise, so visiting the local markets became the daily chore. There were no plastic grocery bags that we Americans throw away so easily. I would have given anything for a few of them. Most of the time I had to take my own baskets with me as I walked around avoiding mud puddles or ruts in the open-air markets with its many tables of various kinds of vegetables or grains. Items purchased were wrapped in brown paper or newspaper and put in the basket carried on my arm. Chickens were killed on the spot and wrapped up. I could never get enough nerve to buy a chicken because I couldn't watch them killing it. Strips of beef hung on a string, and pieces were sliced off, including the flies adhering to them. I soon learned that the beef or any meat had to be frozen for a week to kill all the bacteria. Cooking it well was another precaution. Vegetables were soaked in Clorox water. Precautions had to be taken with the food no matter what it was. A great deal of time was taken to filter the drinking water in ceramic containers.

The weather resembled the weather in Washington, D.C., hot and humid. Air conditioners were put to the test all the time in the office and in the apartment. One of my duties was to deliver some papers to the Consulate in another country, so crossing the river on the ferry was an experience not to be taken lightly. The ferry police carried switches and beat the people if they didn't get on the ferry in time or were holding up the rest of the passengers.

Some of the passengers were old and couldn't move quickly. This was a horribly unsafe situation. The trip was short, so upon arrival, I made my way to the Consulate. The furtive look of fear in the eyes of the people was unsettling.

When my business was completed, I hurriedly boarded the ferry and headed for home and safety.

Invitations abounded to attend receptions at embassies where I met people of different nationalities. Mingling with those of other nationalities was fairly easy because of my past experience among the sisters with whom I had lived. The French language was officially used most of the time. During receptions, I tried to juggle a glass in one hand and a plate of hors d'oeuvres in the other while making light conversation. Most African country leaders were noticeable in their robes of gold, red, blue, or any color imaginable. American and European men in suits and ties lined the rooms, engaged in lively conversations. European and American women in long dresses complimented the men. It certainly made the reception area colorful. The African women wore the most gorgeous head turbans, twisted and turned to make them so attractive. Contacts and promises to get together were made

My boss also had numerous receptions, which I attended. I tried to fit in several times by having a drink, a tonic and vodka, and always went home with a headache and upset stomach. After that experience, I decided I could fit in by drinking a soda.

Because of the turmoil that had existed in town in previous years, women had to be careful when wearing gold earrings or wrist watches. Earrings could be ripped out of ears or wrist watches ripped from one's arm on the street. Purses were held tightly. Men did not carry billfolds in their back pockets because they could be quickly removed by a passerby. They learned to carry a small, black bag with any valuables or cash. This fashion began in Africa long before it did in the United States.

I learned how the different offices worked, what was expected of its occupants, and how many long hours of work were expected. We always seem to be on duty. Whenever there was a problem, we were called in, no questions asked. Contact was always made by radio because there were no phones. All of us had a radio call sign. Many times, we called each other on the radio to plan a get-together or a picnic. Picnics and dinners were a common occurrence. My co-workers became my new family, and I depended on them. The new family really bonded by working together and enjoyed socializing with each other. I learned to host dinners and make dishes from scratch. For one event, I bought a pumpkin in the market, mashed it, strained it and made a scrumptious pumpkin pie, adding all the spices.

Nothing stops time, so with all the activities and work, two years flew by. It was time for me to accept another assignment and another country.

Chapter 6

I'm on home leave visiting my family in Colorado Springs. My father had passed away, so I spent time with my mother and two brothers then drove to Denver to see my twin sister.

The cultural change affected me each time I returned to the United States. Everyone was in a hurry. Cars raced down the road. Leftovers from meals were thrown out, and plastic grocery bags were thrown out. I often wondered why people chose to be in such a fast pace. I had found life in Africa so much more meaningful at a slower pace. People enjoyed each other's company and took time to get to know each other. This life seemed like a whirlwind. After a few weeks of this rapid pace, I had to say goodbye to my family, and off I went to Washington, D.C., to prepare for my next assignment.

Preparations were under way with months of supplies of paper goods, canned items, and dry food purchased and shipped. I let the packers do the heavy work. I bought a small car and had it shipped to a small African country, my next destination.

RETURN TO AFRICA, 1981–1983

Once again, I was on a plane heading for Africa. With one tour of duty under my belt, I felt more secure because I knew what I was getting into. The trip was long, but time waits for no one. The plane landed on African soil. A few of the officers' wives met me and drove to my new house, which had a swimming pool. A swimming pool—what a treat—until I found out it had more than one use. I soon found out the water supply was cut off frequently. Water was taken from the swimming pool, boiled, and drank. Swimming in the pool was also done in lieu of baths or showers. The swimming pool became the center of socializing with my co-workers.

Due to the many power outages, I learned how to start and maintain the generator. That was a major feat. Cooking on a fueled gas burner invoked a lot of ingenuity, juggling one pot after another.

I soon learned the proper etiquette in greeting men and women working in the building. The Chief of Station (COS), affected by hay fever, suffered miserably due to dust everywhere. The hot winds blew in dust storms all the time. He and the other officer (a woman) did not always see things the same way, which is not unusual. She eventually left the country, which left the COS and me to run the office. I soon realized that the "old boys' club" was as strong as ever, as evidenced by HQS supporting him in whatever decisions he made. However, the COS and I worked in harmony to get the job done. The Communications (Commo) guys joined us in many dinners and receptions. Whenever the COS went off on vacation, I had to fill in as acting COS. Some of my previous training prepared me for this, and I managed to make decisions as needed.

MARINE BALL

The Marine Ball was a huge event in the embassy, so when that date arrived, all of us were dressed in our best, and off we went to the ball. My date for that ball was a visitor from the States who was working for the United States Agency for International Development (USAID). Tall and good looking, he was pleasant as a date, so both of us enjoyed the meal and dance. The Marines carried a large cake with the words "Congratulations to the Marine Corp" into the ballroom. The gunny cut the first slice. The Marines befriended everyone.

BOAT TRIP TO TIMBUKTU

Mali is landlocked and has a subtropical to arid climate. It is mostly flat, rising to rolling northern plains covered by sand, with savanna around the Niger River in the south. Most of the country lies in the Sahara Desert, which produces a hot, dust-laden harmattan haze, which is common during dry seasons and leads to recurring droughts.

In this African country is the famous Timbuktu. No name brings the splendor of ancient Africa to mind more than Timbuktu, a great city that flourished on a bend in the Niger River for more than four hundred years. Timbuktu is at the end of the camel caravan route that linked sub-Saharan Africa to North Africa and Arabia. Gold, ivory, and kola nuts passed through Timbuktu, but the most important commodity was salt. Caravans hauled salt from nearby mines to trade for gold. Timbuktu began as a trading city, but in time, it developed into the intellectual and spiritual center of West Africa. By 1330, Timbuktu became part of the kingdom of Mali. The great mosque or temple that was built in Timbuktu attracted scholars from as far away as Saudi Arabia.

There are three options to go to Timbuktu: by air, land, or boat. It's not easy to get there by the road, but it's possible with a four-wheel drive or by bus. One of the more adventurous ways of getting to Timbuktu is by camel. For a price, it's possible to tag along with a caravan across the Sahara desert. The most scenic way of transport is by boat, which is the way I chose. Since the boat stopped at many villages along the way, the trip took five days.

Timbuktu is widely used to describe a place that is far away and regarded by many as a myth. In 1983, among African and European passengers, two Americans destined for Timbuktu boarded the triple-deck ship moored on the Niger River. Doris, my cabin companion, a porcelain doll replica, sporting blue laundered jeans and a T-shirt, carried a basket of food in one hand and lugged a suitcase in the other. Hair dyed light brown, manicured hands with pink nails, and blue and white sneakers complemented her attire. Doris, an employee of a government agency, was unknown to me. We worked for different agencies.

Through the grapevine, she heard I was looking for someone to share a "luxury" cabin and expenses on this ship that was completing its last seasonal trip to Timbuktu. The springs in our steps and our bodily appearances denied our forty plus years.

"Doris, are you excited about making this trip?" I asked.

"Yes, somewhat," she replied.

"It should be a fun trip," I said.

"I've never been on an African ship before."

"I haven't, either, but it's a large ship, so we'll have plenty of room. Do you think you brought enough clothes?"

"Probably not," she replied. My initial contact with Doris in the early stages of preparation was cordial. We seemed compatible.

The sun was just rising for another hot, dry day in Bamako, but no one noticed as the activity going on down at the dock was untiring. Sweat rolled down the faces of people who were lugging their baggage. Others were busy with chickens in makeshift cages. Water bottles and buckets of water were carried onto the ship for the trip. Along with the other passengers, Doris and I dragged suitcases and heaved buckets of water, food, and sunhats to our "luxury cabin." In this cabin, the suitcases had to remain packed because of the small space. There were no rods on which to hang the clothes.

The only piece of furniture in the cabin was a double-deck wooden bed. Doris plopped her suitcase on the lower one. The buckets of water didn't fit into the small bathroom so they, too, had to be placed in the small area. We couldn't do anything else in the cabin.

"Doris, do you want to go to the dining room for lunch?"

"No, I prefer to stay here in the cabin," she said with face flushed.

"Shall I bring you some food?"

"No, I have some with me."

I shrugged my shoulders, thought it odd, and walked down the deck and found my way down to the dining room.

I walked into the dining room. Rows of long tables greeted me in "family style." A gray-haired couple beckoned me to join them.

"Bon jour, Madam. Comment ca va?"

"I'm fine, thank you. Where do you folks come from?"

We exchanged names, and I found out that they had come from Paris just to take this trip. We conversed in French about the boat and what we might expect along the way. They were so interested in the African culture and wanted to get to know the people. While we talked, the aroma of the bowls of stewed beef and rice diverted my attention. The stewed beef was seasoned with some unfamiliar spices but tasted good. Little did we know that beef and rice would be the main dish for most of the trip. Some fruit was also passed around on the tables. I explained to the couple about coming on the trip with a lady from another government agency.

"Where is your friend?" they asked.

"She wanted to remain in the cabin."

While we were meeting other people and enjoying the meal, the Malian crew manned their stations, and the ship churned on its motors. After what seemed to be an eternity of waiting, the ship's motors roared into action, and with a great deal of noise, we left the hot, dusty town of Bamako in the distance.

After the meal I strolled on the deck, but it didn't seem to faze me that it was one hundred and twenty degrees out there. The experience of being present in this moment of time was exhilarating. I was heading for a place few Europeans or Americans ever saw but only heard about.

Martha on deck en route to Timbuktu

As the passengers mingled and met each other the first day on the decks, new friends were made. Speaking French certainly was an asset in communicating with other French-speaking passengers, and soon I became part of their group. Meals were shared as well as off-shore tours into the local market place.

Martha on deck

On the first day, I began to worry about Doris because she remained in the cabin. I thought she must be getting tired of her own food, so I asked her to join me for the noon meal.

"No thanks, I'll just stay here. I'm okay," she said. Again her refusal baffled me.

Since this was the last trip of the season up the Niger River and the water level was so low, the sandbars controlled our destiny. On our first day out on the river, the ship hit sandbars and all engines stopped. The water rocked us from side to side like a mother rocks her infant child. Perspiration dripped down my face despite the shielding sunhat. Other passengers wiped their foreheads. Doris, alarmed, burst out of the cabin.

"What happened? Why have we stopped?"

"We're stuck on the sandbars, and the only thing we can do is wait for a motor boat from Bamako to pull us out."

"How long will that take?"

"The crew said a small motor boat from Bamako will take a day or so."

Under sunglasses her eyebrows arched in bewilderment. Her slight figure brusquely retreated into the cabin.

Time stood still. As the ship swayed for the entire day, the sweat rolled off our faces because of the hot wind. Hats seemed to be a thin veneer to protect from the sun beating down on us. Caught in this stalemate situation, the suffocating heat seemed to smother us. The arid wind blew, and the accompanying sun's scorching rays searched for prey. In this time-stalled moment, we had nowhere to go. Decks stretched to the limit accommodating the various animals and bags of grain. Inactivity and tacit acceptance of fate heightened our helplessness. The hot sun's rays were unmerciful.

The Malians, accustomed to this heat, settled in for their afternoon siesta. Surrender to the elements heightened our plight of inactivity. Hour by hour crept by in the silence of time. The hot and stuffy night air robbed us of sleep.

In the morning, I asked Doris, who was ashen, "Are you all right?" Would you like to walk around a bit?"

"No, I'll just stay here," she said.

I thought she must be claustrophobic by now. "You might like to eat some beef and rice," I said. She remained in the cabin.

To our utter relief, we heard the crew shouting in late afternoon, "The boat from Bamako is here!" A small motor boat came along, and its crew attached ropes to our ship. After a sputtering of motors, it pulled us out of the sandbars.

Many faces broke into smiles. Passengers and crew burst into song and shouts of joy as the water parted with the ship's motors surging full speed ahead. Even the animals seem to make their own noises of joy. Our famous final destination was once again in sight.

Stopping about half mile off shore at different towns along the way brought the African people out to the ship in their small dugouts. Many of the villagers waded out into the water to sell fruit and a variety of foods in baskets balanced on top of their heads. The baskets were pulled up with ropes that had been dropped over the side of the ship. Food was put in and pulled up to the thirsty or hungry recipients. Smiling faces met us everywhere.

Villagers bringing food to boat

The women laughed and spontaneously broke into melodious songs. The melodies invited everyone on the ship to tap feet or clap hands in rhythm.

Women and children wading out to boat with food

The men rowed their small boats out to the ship, and the crew pulled up the food with their ropes from which the ship's crew loaded food for the passengers' meals.

Not only did the ship take on more and more passengers, but chickens, goats, sheep, and bags of grains and supplies were loaded on the ship in every available space. At times, the smell was overwhelming. The deck's being claimed by all the animals made it impossible to walk around. I wanted to go to the end of the deck, but to maneuver about the deck, I had to climb over chicken cages or tied-up goats. The goats weren't too pleased, either, to have people walking around them or pushing them to another place. Their unintelligible voices were easily heard. The caged chickens cackled. Men and women sat in between the cages. Bags of grain destined for the markets literally covered most of the remaining space.

Luxury boat to Timbuktu

The days meshed one into the other with little or nothing to do. We followed a daily routine of eating what food there was and tried to sleep at night, but the heat never relented. I brought a few books along, so I had time to read and relax. Doris stayed in the cabin most of the time.

Villagers standing on shore waiting for boat to arrive

On the last day, the boat pulled into the shore of Timbuktu. I wondered where Timbuktu was. The villagers waved and sang as we disembarked. A few huts dotted the land, but where was the city? This was the city. Miles and miles of sand in every direction in the crushing heat seemed to be a view from another planet. From the edge of the small town, there was nothing to see except a sea of sand. A writer's imagination left to wonder in amazement.

Doris and I walked off the boat with our suitcases. With our sandaled feet, we trudged in sand, which made it uncomfortable and difficult to walk to the hotel. The hotel's open door invited us into a structure made of mud/sand facing a row of mosquito-net covered beds on a floor of sand. The musty, stale smell turned up noses. The air was pungent but tolerable. Because there weren't many windows, our eyes had to adjust to the darkened room. Doris took off her sunglasses and rolled her eyes. Her pink manicured nails covered her mouth, and her eyebrows arched in disgust. A gasp escaped her lips. We looked at each other and decided to accept the inevitable. This was going to be our place to stay for a few days, so we had to get used to it. Both of us walked to the beds and put down our suitcases. She chose one, and I chose the other, which was separated by mosquito netting. A small nightstand stood by each bed with a kerosene lamp and some candles. Doris walked down to the only bathroom.

A few seconds later I heard a shriek coming from that direction. I trudged in the sand as fast as I could to another culture's idea of a bathroom and found a gecko on guard.

"Don't worry, geckos are harmless," I said.

She looked at me with a big question mark in her eyes.

"The geckos do a great job eating insects. They kept the walls in my house in Bamako clean of creeping, crawling things. They won't harm you."

For a toilet there was a hole in the ground that served as the commode, common in Africa. Fascinated by the sink, I washed my hands and feet at the same time as the brown water ran from the faucet to several holes at the base of the broken sink onto my feet. Mom and Dad never had anything like this on the farm. Gathering our sunhats and sunglasses, we headed to the open-air market. The Grande Marche was a covered market in the old section of town. There wasn't a lot of food, but we found cloth, pots and pans, and rock salt from the desert. Rows of Malian women, covered in multi-colored clothes from head to toe, sat on the ground selling their spices and blankets

The huts in Timbuktu were built from a mixture of sand, water, and mud. Hand-made huts, built in a maze, behind the women marketing their wares, completed the painting of this unrealistic part of the world. The maze of walls surrounding the huts protected the people behind the market and kept the wind and dust out to a certain extent. These people selling their wares were covered from head to toe as protection from the merciless sun.

Marketplace in Timbuktu

A painter could not have shown more in his brush strokes than the eye could see. On our return to the hotel, my eyes were glued to the desert of sand. I felt I was in a movie as a caravan of Bedouins, riding on their camels, approached closer and closer. Mesmerized by this moment, I imprinted the scene on my memory. Disbelieving, I watched the Bedouins advance, clothed in black from head to toe, atop their camels. In movies, how many times had I been an outsider to a scene like this? Now I was an actual player. As I watched the caravan approach, one of the Bedouins asked, "Would you like to ride my camel?"

Well, since I had never been on a camel before, I stepped forward and said, "Yes, I would."

The Bedouin spoke a few words to the camel, and he slowly bent his long legs and knelt down. I stepped nearer, put my foot on the stirrup, and pulled myself up. Then I hung on for dear life when the camel stood up and I was higher than I cared to be. The camel turned his head to me and tried to bite me. The Bedouin laughed and said, "He probably doesn't like you."

The camel decided to walk a few steps, but that was enough for me. The orders were given to the camel to kneel, and I got off. The camel didn't like a different rider, as evidenced by his attempt to bite me. I readily gave my place to someone else. After some time, the Bedouins displayed their wares that they had brought to sell at the market. The man, whose camel I had ridden, showed me two swords that were made of copper.

"I will give you a good price to buy these," he said. I looked them over and really liked what I saw.

"How much?" I asked.

He quoted a price. Money was brought out, and I became the new owner of two swords in their leather cases.

Martha on camel in Timbuktu

Because it was so late in the season and since our ship had to be towed out of the sandbars, the ship returning to Bamako was cancelled. The only other means of transport back to Bamako was the plane. We checked in with the police to get our passports stamped with the Timbuktu stamp. The officer notified my employer of the reason for my delay in returning to work. We followed directions to the airlines to make a plane reservation for the next plane out to Bamako. The airline official—there was only one airline official—informed us of the one flight to Bamako the next day. Flights regularly failed to materialize, stranding passengers for days.

Doris and I were at the airport early the next day, and we boarded the only flight.

"I'm glad to be going home," Doris said. "It has been a difficult trip for me because I had to make a decision about whether to remain for another tour of duty or return to the States. I appreciate your not pressuring me for answers or to join you for meals. I have decided to return to the States and

71

work there. I enjoyed most of the trip and enjoyed meeting you. Thank you for everything."

"I enjoyed the trip, too," I said.

The plane landed, and we parted company and went our separate ways with a few grains of sand still in our clothing and in our hair and the stamp of the famous Timbuktu in our passports.

Nothing could ever be comparable to a trip to Timbuktu, where nature's elements and people from an unreal world really do exist.

AFRICA, TEMPORARY DUTY, 1983

With my two-year assignment completed, I returned to the States. Before my next PCS (Permanent Change of Station) assignment, I was asked to take a TDY (Temporary Duty) to another African country, and I agreed. The assignment would take about six weeks, so after obtaining the proper visas, I was on an airplane again heading for Africa.

One day while working in the small office, the whole building shook as an earthquake raised its ugly head. No one was hurt, but the sensation of moving and not being able to stop was frightening.

This country was a French-speaking country, but English was spoken in the workplace. With my rental car, I drove down the road but had to watch out for camels on the road. Where else would one have to watch out for camels on the road?

Camel on road

Chapter 7

AFRICA, 1984–1986, GOVERNMENT WORKER

In the year 1984, Ronald Reagan was re-elected president of the United States. In this same year, I was again in Africa. This particular country was a little different from my previous assignments. The majority of the people were Muslims, so at the appropriate time, no matter where they were, they would get down on their knees and pray to Allah. It was a common sight to see the men and women in long, white, flowing robes kneel and bow their head to the ground. It reminded me of the time I had been a nun and had to pray at certain times. We went to a chapel to pray, but nevertheless, we followed times of prayer as did these people.

In this country, the higher altitude and cooler weather made for a pleasant stay. I began work every day by passing through security maintained by the guards. Opening the door combination, I found a desk and chair, filing cabinets, and a window air conditioner greeting me each day. The office to the left was for the COS, and the other, to the right, for an officer. One official's office was a short walk down the hall. I frequented it daily with important documents. There were other people working in this building, so we often met for picnics and get-togethers and generally enjoyed our time away from the office. But we were always on call.

Having the office building only a few miles from my home made it possible for me to drive home for lunch. The guard opened the gate as I drove up to the two-bedroom house, which was surrounded by a high wall topped with cut glass. I enjoyed this house because it had a large living room, a dining room, and a large kitchen. The yard around the house proved to be a resting place for many fruit trees, especially banana trees.

For this assignment, I had brought with me a small dog, a Spitz (American Eskimo), and named him Coconut. He was such a delight to have. In the house, I kept the air conditioner working day and night because of the heat during the day and for the little dog, which had a coat of thick white hair. The maid and house guard also took care of the dog and loved playing with him. They had never seen a dog with so much hair. Coconut and I would go on walks down the road, but I always watched out for other animals.

The maid had a big job because the wind stirred up the dust on the dirt roads, so cleaning the furniture was a major task. She cleaned the house, kept it spotless, and cooked for me at times when I came home for lunch and a siesta.

"Madam, it's time to get up," she would say. I always got back to work on time.

When I arrived home from work, Coconut came running to greet me, curled tail wagging. That little white fluffy dog was a wonderful companion. I paid the guard to take special care of him because of the many snakes surrounding the area.

Martha and Coconut

Because the guard was used to catching snakes in the village, watching out for them around my house was nothing new. One day the guard saw a snake crawling into the house. He had the ability to catch a snake by its tail and snap its neck before it got a chance to bite.

I drove up the driveway so the guard could let me in the gate. He said, "Madam, I caught this green mamba crawling into the house before it got to Coconut."

I am deathly afraid of snakes, so I looked as he showed it to me, but I didn't get too close.

When I returned to the office, I told the officers about the snake. A few phone calls were made, and the snake, because of its size, was on its way to Paris to a museum.

SATURDAY OUTING

On Saturday mornings, a group from work joined together for a walk. An official, living near me, asked if I would drive him to the meeting place for the walk. Coconut was used to the front seat, so when the official got in on the passenger side, I said, "I'm sorry, but you're sitting in the dog's place."

He laughingly said, "Oh, that's all right. I'll hold him."

So my dog sat proudly on his lap. Coconut showed his respect and thanks by licking him over and over. We met the others at the meeting place. The walk was refreshing with the cool air in the morning and the picturesque view of the mountains as a backdrop. We walked a few miles to the top of the hill and relaxed in the restaurant with a cool drink before heading back down to the bottom of the hill. It was a time to enjoy a walk and talk about things other than business.

Food had to be purchased, so in this country, as in others, a trip to the market to buy food was an adventure and a challenge. I often went to the open-air market to buy fruit and veggies with my basket on my arm. As I mentioned on a previous page, I never bought a chicken because I couldn't watch its throat being sliced. Meat was laid on a table for me to choose the piece or pieces desired and wrapped in newspaper. Precautions had to be taken, as in other countries, so it had to be left in the freezer for a week or so in order for it to cure and to get rid of the bacteria and bugs.

There was a grocery store, but all the items were imported from other countries, which raised the prices. Bread called "baguettes" was plentiful and could be purchased any time of the day at a local shop. The aroma alone led one to the shop. This bread was hot and delicious. It was only good the day it came out of the oven and had no preservatives.

FRIENDSHIPS

At different functions, I had met some American teachers at the school. We seemed to have a lot in common, so we became friends. During the times they visited my house, we talked often about our lives and what they had been in the United States. I got to know their two sons and followed their progress though the years. All of us are now back in the United States, but we still correspond with each other. This type of friendship happened often during the years I spent in various African countries. Most of the people with whom

I worked had young families, so following their children through the years by correspondence was a joy for me as well as for the parents. I never would have met such nice, dedicated people if I had not been in Africa. Lasting friendships were formed and continued through the years. I never realized just how important those friendships were until I remained in the States years later. Contact was made by letters because we were scattered throughout the States. Their friendship was priceless and meant a great deal to me.

As with all my other assignments, my two years were coming to a close. This assignment would be my last tour in Africa. My mother had been asking me over and over when I was coming home to stay. She had written many times asking me when I was going to settle down and remain in the States. I told her I had bought a dog, which was the first step, so now I finished my assignments and would be heading back to the States to stay. I don't think she ever felt I was safe all alone in a foreign country, although I had mentioned many times that I had many friends. It was time for me to head home. I knew I wouldn't accept any more foreign assignments but wanted to finish my time in the States and then retire.

My decision was made, so I made arrangements to head back to the States. I was leaving six hundred and eighty million people in Africa who belonged to several thousand different ethnic groups. I had learned a great deal from each country's culture.

I believe I am a much richer person for having had these experiences because I've learned other customs, learned how to adapt to other cultures, learned their languages, and I became a much more well-rounded, understanding person. Each ethnic group has its own distinct language, traditions, arts and crafts, history, way of life, and religion. Perhaps I have made a difference for some of the people and affected their lives for the better.

I was sorry to leave because this continent had been part of my life for the past fourteen years. I had met many wonderful people, and I knew I would always have a place in my heart for Africa. As I left Africa, my hope was that I had made some small contribution to this great continent. My dream to work in Africa had been realized in so many ways, which will always influence my words, deeds, and actions in relating to others. It truly had been a life-changing experience and priceless in its richness.

My future plans were to remain in Washington, D.C., until I completed my twenty years with the agency and then to retire in Denver, Colorado.

Chapter 8

DECISION TO REMAIN IN WASHINGTON, D.C., 1986–1998

Back in the States, I found a townhome in Sterling, Virginia, and moved in with Coconut. Until retirement, my remaining years were spent in the Washington, D.C. area. My job at the agency was in the Finance and Accounting Department in Langley, Virginia, at the CIA headquarters building and in other buildings. A lot of things had changed since I had left—new buildings, new parking lots, and lots of new people. As I got used to the fast pace again, numerous classes were added to my schedule during the following twelve years.

In my townhouse, my two dogs, Coconut and Claudia, a new addition, became the delight of the neighborhood children. When we walked around the small park in the neighborhood, the children ran up to me and asked if they could pet my dogs. Coconut and Claudia, a beige terrier-type mixture, wagged their tails and enjoyed the attention. I decided to get a second dog because I was at work for so many hours, and Coconut was always alone. He needed company.

Martha with Coconut and Claudia

Because my mother had always encouraged me to get a dog to settle down, I did, but I got two. As the owner of these dogs, my decision to remain in the States was cemented. I would not travel with two dogs, and I wanted to remain in the States to possibly get my four-year degree. Well, that didn't happen because it was so expensive to live in the D.C. area, and I worked a lot of overtime to make ends meet.

I hadn't been around family for so many years, so I thought it would be better to remain near D.C., even though they lived in Colorado and other states.

Driving the sixteen miles to work in Langley gave me time to breathe the fresh air and enjoy the manicured horse farms along the way with their many well-fed horses. The large, luxury homes made me wonder who the occupants were, what they were doing, and what kind of family life they had.

It was during this same year that the Challenger Space Shuttle exploded. What a tragedy for so many people and their families. The United States bombed Libya, and the IRA-contra scandal broke. The world was going through many changes, which were also echoed in my life. I had worked in Africa for so many years, and now I had to learn how to live in my own country. I had never had a car with power steering or power brakes. I had to learn all this while others took it for granted. Computers became the means to get work done, so that was another hurdle to overcome. I had to remember to keep to the right side of the road, and often times, I was confused as to which side of the car to get into. I was so used to driving on the left with the right side steering wheel.

WORK DIFFERENCES

Working in Langley and working in Africa were worlds apart. In Langley, the offices were busy. People didn't have time for each other, and work was the predominant focus of the day. Adjusting to this timetable and the fast-paced environment shook my world because I had been used to a slower pace with people caring for people. Circumstances now were so different. I immersed myself in my work, and then drove home and enjoyed my dogs. The summers were long, hot, and humid, and the winters, cold and humid. The snow-packed roads made it difficult to drive. I really looked forward to retiring. I knew I would pack up and move to Colorado.

During my last few months, as retirement came nearer and nearer, I wanted to do something for my friends who had helped me through the years. Two of them I had met while sitting in the waiting room, waiting to be interviewed during those first days with the CIA. So I planned something and then told them about it. They were so surprised and pleased because no one had ever done this type of thing before.

My last planned event in Washington, D.C., was to rent a limo and take four of my friends and Lois, my sister-in-law, Sig, Jr.'s widow, (who had arrived to accompany me on my trip to Colorado) for a last ride to say goodbye to the Jefferson Memorial, Lincoln Memorial, Kennedy Center, Arlington Cemetery, the White House, and the Capitol Building. They all came to my house, and when the sleek black limo pulled up in front of my home, shouts of glee interrupted casual chatter. One by one, we climbed into the luxurious stretched-out car for the twenty-mile ride to the downtown area.

"Martha, we'll never forget this. How did you ever think of doing something like this?" asked one of my friends.

I smiled and said, "Well, I wanted to leave D.C. with a memory I wouldn't forget. "Lois, would you like to drink a soda?"

"Yes, I would, thanks," she answered. We had soft drinks in the car and enjoyed every minute of the ride downtown. Laughter and lively talk were non-stop along the way. Each time we got out to view one of the monuments, people stared at us and pointed to the car. Cameras clicked, proving their worth with bulbs flashing and shutters clicking.

"This is so much fun. I am so pleased Martha is doing this for us," one of my friends said.

They chatted happily and consumed the sodas provided whenever they got back into the limo. I think my joy was greater than theirs because I could treat them for their warm friendship through the years. The memorable trip ended, and we were back at my house. One by one, my friends said, "Martha, thank you so much for this wonderful day. We enjoyed ourselves so much and won't forget this. Have a safe trip home and don't forget us."

They knew I wouldn't. We hugged and kissed each other. A perfect day had come to an end. This was my final farewell to the historical city of D.C. Later in the evening, Lois and I prepared to leave in the morning en route for her daughter's home in North Carolina.

VISITS ON THE WAY TO COLORADO

My house was sold, and my bags were packed. Lois and I loaded the car. Claudia jumped in, and off we headed to Colorado via North Carolina. Sadly, I had had to have Coconut put down due to illness and disease. It was one of the most difficult times of my life to lose him. He had been with me in Africa and had been such a faithful companion. I missed him terribly.

We started out early in the morning and drove all day until late at night when we arrived in North Carolina. The winding road led up into the mountains where my niece, Sherry, lived in an old home, which she wanted to eventually turn into a bed and breakfast. Claudia was happy to get out of the car and played well with their two large dogs. The family had prepared a wonderful steak dinner for us, so after a lot of catching up, we finally headed to our beds. The visit was short, but bonds were cemented.

The following day Lois, Claudia, and I headed for Haysville, Kansas, to visit Lois' son, Steve, and his family. After meeting all the family members, dinner was a family sharing. I had planned that we would stay only one day at each family home, so early the next day, we were on the road again heading for Denver, my final destination.

PERMANENT RESIDENCE, DENVER, COLORADO, 1998

We arrived in Denver, and Mary, my twin sister, welcomed us into her two-story home. Lois and I were tired, and Claudia was happy to lie down and sleep on the floor. Mary had prepared a nice dinner for us. I was happy to be back in Colorado. Lois was eager to get back to her home in Oregon, and she left the next morning on a plane. She had been a great traveling companion and was pleased to have seen her daughter and son on the way.

Adjusting to the freedom of retirement, I began searching for a house. Weeks and weeks of visiting homes wasn't exactly my cup of tea, but after seeing so many not to my liking or price range, I finally decided on a new ranch model being built. In the meantime, I stayed with Mary. Two of her three children were married and had their own homes. Her eldest son had died a few months before from a heart attack. I had flown home for the funeral. I knew she had never gotten over his death and still grieved.

When the house was built and the paperwork completed, I became a proud homeowner and moved in my household effects, ready, once again, to begin a new phase of my life. It took a lot of unpacking, putting dishes away, putting things in bedrooms, and setting up the living room. I enjoyed a two-car garage all to myself. Since I was the first occupant, the house smelled new in every room.

THE NARFE ORGANIZATION

The weeks went by, and I began to wonder what I was going to do with my time until I saw a newspaper ad about a federal retirees' meeting of the National Active and Retired Federal Employees Association (NARFE). I called the number in the paper but finally ended up going to the meeting two months later and was warmly welcomed by a couple, George and Shirley Magnuson, and JoDell McDonald, who remain my dear friends today. George and Shirley were so friendly and came over to the table where I was sitting and said, "Welcome to our meeting. We're happy you came here." JoDell also greeted me. Little did I know then that I would end up being the chapter president with George as my secretary. My life story is finished because of JoDell's persistent encouragement to complete this book.

George Magnuson receiving an award from Martha

JoDell McDonald

At every meeting thereafter, these same people made me feel welcome, and I learned about the organization. It originated in 1921 to protect the earned rights and benefits of federal workers, retirees, and survivor annuitants. This interested me. I called the members on my list to remind them of the upcoming meeting. The following year I ran for the treasurer's office and was elected. A year after that, I was elected chapter president.

As president of a chapter, I had to prepare the agenda for my meetings, find program speakers, and generally make sure everything ran smoothly for the monthly meetings. Other times, there were training sessions to attend and federation executive board meetings, which I also attended. I soon got to meet a lot of other members from other chapters. The federation president asked me to be a member of a committee or chair a different committee, and I accepted. I was beginning to feel very comfortable in the organization and hoped I was making a contribution. My plans were to continue working for this organization because whatever I had given, the return had been a hundredfold.

The following is an account of my life-threatening experience and shows how the organization helped to keep me grounded and heal at the same time.

LIFE-THREATENING ILLNESS

In November 2001, Mary and I planned to go to lunch after my annual mammogram appointment. I heard the usual advice from the nurse.

"Undress to the waist. When you're ready, come into this room."

I had been through this many times. After the crushing torture, as I called it, the nurse told me to wait on the chair outside the room while she developed the x-ray and the radiologist read it. Waiting for the results of this mammogram took longer than usual. She returned and asked, "Martha, would you come in again? I have to take a few more x-rays."

I followed her back into the room, and she did some more crushing. When she returned, face stoic but friendly, I knew something was wrong.

"The radiologist wants to speak with you," she said. My heart thumped. I had put on the gown in the brightly-colored changing room, which I had noticed earlier, but now I saw nothing. I focused only on her words.

My twin sister, of 61 years, sat in the lavender-appointed waiting room oblivious to my alarm. The doctor asked for family members to be present, so Mary was called in. Surprised and bewildered, she looked at me with eyebrows arched, her left hand clutching her purse.

Mary

I had come to Denver to retire and get reacquainted with her. We spent a lot of time together. Perhaps, it was fate that she accompanied me that day. We were escorted into the darkened room, and the radiologist looked at my x-rays. He pointed to a mass and said, "There's a suspicious mass, which I believe is cancerous. I suggest you contact a surgeon as soon as possible."

Disbelief was easier to assimilate than reality. Mary and I walked out of the building. I said to her, "This can't be happening to me."

Her hazel eyes filled with tears. For fourteen years I had lived and worked in Africa, where disease was rampant. I had had hepatitis from impure drinking water. I had suffered with parasites, and I had endured loneliness, hardship, danger, and untold stress. Now, in the great United States of America, I was told I had cancer. I couldn't believe those words. I kept saying over and over to Mary, "It can't be happening to me."

I had had no symptoms. Reality hit hard, so I had to make arrangements. After a short lunch we stopped at my primary doctor's office, and after explaining what was happening, the nurse gave me a referral to a surgeon. I still couldn't believe this was happening to me. I didn't feel sick, and I had no symptoms. The next day, Mary went with me to see the surgeon. After feeling the tumor, he confirmed the diagnosis. "I'm 99 percent sure it's malignant. Do you want a biopsy first?" he asked.

"No, do what you have to do," I said.

"We'll set you up for surgery."

Another patient had cancelled for Monday, so I was scheduled for that day. My plans were to attend a NARFE budget meeting that day, but I had to cancel.

I squandered the next two days in denial. Simple daily tasks like getting up in the morning, eating breakfast, and feeding the dog were performed routinely, not conscious actions. How would the diagnosis and subsequent treatment affect my life? My body didn't feel differently. The frightening incident happened too fast. I lacked time to assimilate the impact, the enormity of the disease or its consequences. Time stood still for me to experience the gamut of emotions. Numbness engulfed my mind and body. Action was my next avenue of defense.

On Saturday, the next day, Mary and I were invited to our brother's place in Colorado Springs to celebrate his fiftieth wedding anniversary. When we arrived, some of the family members were already there. While we were all talking, my sister-in-law, Kay, pulled me aside.

"Martha, are you all right?" she asked. "You look so pale."

I tearfully blurted out the news. She immediately said she and Lee would come to Denver to be with me for the surgery. Having family around was a new experience because I had been alone for so many years and never had family members to help me. I had gone through five surgeries alone in Washington, D.C., and was alone during the recuperation period. It hadn't been easy, but when you're alone, you do for the best. I asked Kay not to say anything until after Mary and I left for Denver.

On Monday morning, with Lee and Kay and Mary in the waiting room, I was the one prepped in the white gown. They came in to see me.

"Martha, are you okay?"

"I guess so. I have to be. I can't change anything, so it's all out of my hands."

Several of the doctors and technicians came in and explained what they were going to do to me. One after the other told me this or that, and finally it all became a blur. I guess they were all ready because someone else came in and gave me an injection in my back, which put me in slumber land. The surgery took a few hours, and after the surgery, I woke up in the hospital room with terrible pain in my left arm. I said to the nurse, "My arm hurts so much."

The doctors must have laid my arm in an awkward position because the intense pain prevented sleep. The nurse finally brought in a pillow and put it under my arm and gave me a pain pill. I wasn't aware of any other pain except the pain in my arm, and I knew the doctor didn't operate on my arm. When the surgeon came in, he told me what he had done.

"I performed a lumpectomy, a breast-sparing surgery, so I didn't have to take the whole breast," he said.

The endless treatments, needles, and blood tests began.

I spent a few days in the hospital and was glad to leave it. After being released from the hospital, I had Mary by my side, helping me change bandages. A tube was inserted into my breast with a small container for drainage at the other end. This was attached to my nightgown.

"Mary, help me empty this tube."

She took the small container hooked to my nightgown and emptied it.

"There was quite a bit of blood in it this time," she said. This container had to be emptied every few hours, so she stayed with me. I couldn't lift my arm because lymph nodes had been removed and it was dreadfully sore.

"Martha, you have to eat something. I'll make some soup for you."

I really didn't care to eat anything but forced myself to take a spoonful. At other times, she brought me a chocolate milkshake, which I liked.

Gradually, after a couple of weeks, I grew stronger and managed to get myself up without any help. The time was coming to take the chemo. Mary drove me to the office where the nurse hooked me up to the needles. I refused to get a port near my shoulder blade, so she had to put the needle in a vein in my hand. As I sat on the easy chair and watched the drip flow for an hour and forty-five minutes, I wondered what this medication was doing to my system. During the drip, I didn't feel sick.

"Martha, do you want something to read?"

"No, I don't feel like reading."

She sat in one of the chairs for family members and watched me. I don't know what was going through her mind, but I'm sure she was glad she wasn't sitting in my place. When the treatment was over, Mary drove me home, and I would go to bed to rest. The nausea began even though I had pills to counteract it.

My visits to the oncologist were often for repeated tests, so the nurses specializing in oncology could give me the right dosage of Coumadin, a medication that killed both my red and white blood cells. My immune system was down to nothing, so being careful around people who had colds or allergies was an absolute must. I didn't go out much except to conduct my NARFE meetings.

Mary sat through every chemo session I had to take for six months. After each session, I went home sick. Nausea was a constant companion despite all the pills to counteract it. I read books on cancer, nutrition, and hygiene. I researched coping skills on the internet when I had my good days. What would chemo do to my system, and how would I react to it? Would I lose my hair like so many others had? I delved into information on radiation. A representative from the Cancer Society had given me booklets pertaining to treatment and consequences. I was encouraged to join a support group, but I never did. I guess I didn't because I just did not feel well enough to exert energy. During my life, I had gone through so many events and illnesses alone.

NARFE MEETINGS

My NARFE chapter meeting was in the beginning of the month, so I always scheduled my chemo treatment after that because I knew I would be worthless for the remainder of the month. By the time I felt well enough, the next treatment squashed that feeling. But it was a fact that I had to focus on preparing my meeting agenda and to arrange for speakers and programs. I credit NARFE for saving my life. I had to keep my mind focused on NARFE issues and not on myself. I don't believe many of my chapter members knew I was going through chemo because I never lost my hair and had no outward signs except fatigue. Fatigue played a huge part, but I managed to get through the meetings.

My next challenge arose with the formation of a blood clot in my leg. The oncologist prescribed Coumadin again, a blood thinner. During this time, my fear heightened with the numerous blood tests taken. If results from a blood test showed my blood level was low, it necessitated a change in dosage. Advised by the nurses to increase or decrease the Coumadin subjected my body to constant change.

After a long six months, the chemo treatments ended. Radiation was about to begin. Daily, for seven weeks, I sat in the waiting room in my oversized dressing gown to be taken in the special room so infrared beams could burn into my body.

"Good morning, how are you today?" the nurse asked.

Was I supposed to say I was doing fine? I always answered, "I'm okay." I was taken into a room where a huge machine sprayed its rays over me. Radiation also caused acute fatigue.

One complication followed another, and I faced a new challenge— radiation burn. I wondered what else could happen. I was treated with antibiotics, which finally cleared up the infection. The doubt of ever being healthy again lurked in my mind.

During the following year, I went to the emergency room and was admitted with high fever and a swollen arm with blisters all over it. Lymphedema and cellulites grew in my arm, a result of the removal of twenty-two lymph nodes during my cancer surgery. To what extent my stamina could withstand or be tested by an illness became a never-ending question.

Gradually, I did get stronger and stronger and eventually was told I was in remission. Remission may be an unimportant word, but to me, and to many who have had cancer, the word is golden. The fear of recurring cancer is always there in the back of my mind, but life goes on, and I have to make the best of it. I felt healthy again and felt good.

Mary's Death

One day early in the morning, I called Mary. "Have you had breakfast yet?" I asked.

"No."

"I'll come over and bring you breakfast," I said. I stopped at a fast food restaurant and bought our breakfast and headed for her home.

"Oh good, you brought bacon and eggs," she said. She loved her bacon. She made some coffee, so we enjoyed our bacon and eggs together.

"I'm going over to my neighbor's to pick some grapes, so I'll bring you some later," she said

I went home, and around noon, she arrived with a bucket of grapes.

"I feel tired, so I'm going home," she said. Later in the evening, her daughter phoned me asking where her mom was because she had promised to baby-sit and hadn't arrived. I told her I had had breakfast with her mom in the morning but didn't know where she was. I suggested she go over to her mother's home and check on her, which she did. She called back sobbing. Her mom was on the floor, unconscious, and she couldn't wake her. She called the ambulance. I drove to the hospital and asked questions about my sister.

My niece and her husband and children arrived, so we were all ushered into a room. About an hour later, we were given the news that Mary could not be revived. She had died of a pulmonary thrombosis. It was a very bleak day. It was not easy to understand this because I had been the one who had been ill. Mary had been so good to me during my illness, and now she was gone.

My niece made arrangements for the funeral, which brought my younger sister, Minny, from Texas and my two brothers, Lee and Josh, from Colorado Springs to Denver. Walking down the isle of the church and seeing the picture of Mary was too much for me. Tears streamed down my face, and I let out a cry. Minny and Lee came around and helped me to my place in the church. Somehow I managed to get through the funeral and the burial. Twins have a special bond, and when that bond is severed, the loss is great. It was such a huge loss for me. Time heals but leaves a hole that is never replenished.

Three months later my brother, Linus (Josh), passed away, so once again, the family was brought together. My brother, Lee, and my younger sister, Minny, and I met in Colorado Springs, where Josh was buried. Out of six siblings, only three of us remain. My oldest brother, Sig Jr., had passed away in 1994. My father passed away in 1978, and my mother, in 1995.

Family, front: L-R Martha, Mom, Dad, Mary.
Back: L-R, Linus, Minny, Leroy, Sig Jr.).

Experiences Summarized

Life experiences continue. I've experienced some health problems since then and will continue to have them, according to the doctors. As the prey of a life-threatening or life-challenging illness, I realized no matter how much support was given by family, friends, or organizations, I had to face the disease with all its treatments and complications alone. This type of illness changed my attitude toward life, with energy now being placed on the important, leaving the unimportant to take care of itself. For the past nine years, I have been a survivor. A survivor. What is a survivor? You could say it's one who "weathers the storm." The words "you have breast cancer" are probably the most devastating four words a woman or man can hear. How did I get through all this turmoil? I lived each day as if it were my last. I prayed a lot and tried to keep a positive attitude by focusing on the good happening in my life. I accepted each day's challenges, small as they were. There is a rainbow after the frightening storm. I had to look for it. Some days I found it; other days I didn't.

NARFE has played a major role in my life. I came up through the ranks from chapter treasurer, chapter president to federation first vice president, and then to federation president and was re-elected for a second term.

Martha addressing Colorado convention delegates

Martha addressing the delegates

After two and half years as the Colorado federation president, I was elected by the five states, Arizona, Colorado, New Mexico, Utah, and Wyoming to be regional vice president, the office I continue to hold today. The duties entail traveling to the different states and attend federation executive board meetings as well as district training meetings. I also travel to our headquarters in Virginia to attend national executive board meetings.

In 2006, I had been appointed by the then national president to chair the resolutions committee at a national convention in Albuquerque, New Mexico. It was a frightening but exhilarating experience to stand before fifteen hundred people and present information. In 2008, the national president appointed me, as a member of the national executive board, to be on the site selection committee, so I traveled to different cities to check out hotels for the upcoming national convention in 2014.

I have made another potential life-changing decision. For the 2010 national convention, I was a candidate for the national vice president's position but did not win the election. It was a close race.

I have received numerous awards, including the Meritorious, Distinguished Service Award and the prestigious Hall of Fame Award, the highest award given in Colorado.

I was featured in the October 2005 issue of the NARFE magazine. St. Anthony Hospital's magazine, *Vim & Vigor,* also featured my life story in spring of 2007. I am a participant in the St. Anthony Health Foundation,

Flight for Life. The foundation offered me the opportunity during one of their training sessions to act as an accident patient. One of the hospital staff members prepared me with actual painted and realistic head and leg injuries resulting from a motorcycle accident. I was loaded into the Flight for Life helicopter and flown to St. Anthony's Central hospital, landed on the roof's helipad and rolled on a gurney into the emergency room. The doctors explained to the other participants what emergency action they would take to save my life. It was an enlightening and informative experience to see how much care these dedicated people take to save lives while at the same time risk their own lives.

Flight for Life helicopter

Chapter 9

PLANS FOR THE FUTURE

My plans for the future are to continue working for this organization because whatever I have given on my part, the return has been more than a hundredfold. A great lesson I've learned is that a leader cannot be a leader without followers, faithful, loyal followers.

There are many paths in life that twist and turn because of decisions we make. Mine have led me to work with the people in Africa in various capacities, and now I'm working with retirees and active federal employees to protect our earned benefits. In order to serve this particular group of people in a broader capacity, I decided to run for the national vice president's position. I ran a close race but didn't win the election at the August/September 2010 national convention in Grand Rapids, Michigan. I'm ready now to begin a new phase in my life.

In summary, I have served as a missionary nun for seventeen years in Africa, and in the States, I worked for the Central Intelligence Agency for twenty years in Africa and in the States. Since retirement, I have worked with NARFE for twelve years in Denver, Colorado.

Because of my many different life experiences, both in Africa and in the States, NARFE provides me the opportunity to help people understand that there is someone fighting for them to protect their benefits. I have helped people in Africa, learned a new culture, new languages, and in the States, became a leader to help others by becoming a conduit of information to help people who have expertise in one area help others. I have learned to be a team player, which no doubt comes from my experiences of being a nun. As a NARFE leader on the regional level, I traveled around to my states and listened to the members, tried to resolve problems, and encouraged them the best I could.

One day as I was busy in my office, the phone rang. I listened to a woman who asked for help to make a decision concerning her health plan.

"Have you tried our retirement section in headquarters?" I asked.

She said she had already done that and was told she had to make the decision herself. She said, "I know I have to make the decision myself, but I need help to make that decision."

I asked where she was located. When she mentioned the city and state, my mind immediately located someone.

"I know someone there who can help you," I told her. I gave her the name and phone number. If I had not had this position and traveled to the various states and met members who helped others, I would not have been able to give her this information. A few days later, she phoned again.

"Thank you so much for giving me that man's name and number. He was so helpful and even came to my home to discuss it with me. I can't tell you how pleased I am because I have now made my decision."

Good news like this makes my day.

My life experiences have taught me to have hope, no matter what life has in store for me. Faith, hope, inner strength, and a dream can carry one farther than anyone can imagine. I am ready to face my future, wherever it may lead.

Bibliography

"American Cultural History—The Twentieth Century, 1940–1949." Kingwood College Library. 28 Oct. 2006._http://kelibrary.nbmccd.edu.decade.40. html.

"Central Intelligence Agency." Wikipedia. 21 Aug. 2009. http://en.wikipedia. org/wiki/Central_Intelligence_Agency.

Dowling, Mike. "Mr. Dowling's Africa Today Page." 9 April 2006. http://www. mrdowling.com/611africatoday.html.

Rosenberg, Jennifer. "Timeline of the Twentieth Century." 1980–1989. 28 Oct. 2006. http://history1900s.about.com/library/time/bltime1980.htm.

"Timbuktu—City of Legends." BBC News Online. 9 April 2006. http://newsbbc. co.uk/I/hi/world/africa/1911321.stm.

"Timbuktu, Mali." The History Channel. 9 April 2006. http://www. historychannel.com/classroom/unesco/timbuktu/bibliography.

"Timeline of United States history (1950–1969)." Wikipedia. 28 Oct. 2006. http://en.wikipedia.org/wiki9/timeline_of_United_States_history_(195.

"Timeline of United States History (1970–1989)." Wikipedia. 28 Oct. 2006. http://en.wikipedia.org/wiki/timeline_of_United_sStates_history_(197.

"Timeline of United States History (1990–present)." Wikipedia. 28 Oct. 2006. http://en.wikipedia.org/wiki/Timeline_of_United_States_history_(1990).

National Active and Retired Federal Employees Association (NARFE). www. narfe.org.

St. Anthony Health Foundation. www.stanthonyhealthfoundation.org